PRAISE FOR

VEGAN CUPCAKES

TAKE OVER THE WORLD

"Packed with 75 dairy-free recipes *and* lush photos aimed at making vegans and omnivores drool." —*Washington Post*

❧

"Written chattily and supportively for even the most oven-phobic . . . reading this is like having a couple of fun, socially conscious post-punk pals over for a slumber party . . . . Each page of this cookbook contains an irresistible delight." —*Bust*

❧

"Work your way up from amateur to vegan cupcake master of the universe." —*VegNews*

❧

"Yep, they're all dairy-free, but do you really want to waste time talking egg substitutes when there are Cappuccino Cupcakes filled with Espresso Crème to be eaten?" —*Gannett News Service*

❧

"If you like sweet things (and who doesn't?) and you're vegan you are seriously missing out if this book doesn't inhabit your kitchen shelf." —SuperVegan.com

❧

"I am giving this amazing cookbook to all my friends! These beautiful cupcakes are delicious and loaded with wonderful ingredients. I can't wait to have a cupcake/champagne party so we can try them all!" —Alicia Silverstone

PRAISE FOR
VEGAN WITH A VENGEANCE

"Plenty of attitude, and killer recipes to back it up. Watch out Betty Crocker."
—Erik Marcus, Vegan.com

❧

"[Features] dairy-free desserts that are tasty enough to fool most omnivores."
—*Publishers Weekly*

❧

"Good, honest vegan recipes with broad appeal." —*Associated Press*

❧

"Creative, inventive and yummy . . . amazingly decadent desserts." —*Herbivore*

PART ONE

HOW TO MAKE KICK-ASS
CUPCAKES

METRIC CONVERSIONS

- The recipes in this book have not been tested with metric measurements, so some variations might occur.
- Remember that the weight of dry ingredients varies according to the volume or density factor: 1 cup of flour weighs far less than 1 cup of sugar, and 1 tablespoon doesn't necessarily hold 3 teaspoons.

General Formulas for Metric Conversion

Ounces to grams	⇒ ounces × 28.35 = grams
Grams to ounces	⇒ grams × 0.035 = ounces
Pounds to grams	⇒ pounds × 453.5 = grams
Pounds to kilograms	⇒ pounds × 0.45 = kilograms
Cups to liters	⇒ cups × 0.24 = liters
Fahrenheit to Celsius	⇒ (°F − 32) × 5 ÷ 9 = °C
Celsius to Fahrenheit	⇒ (°C × 9) ÷ 5 + 32 = °F

Linear Measurements

½ inch = 1½ cm
1 inch = 2½ cm
6 inches = 15 cm
8 inches = 20 cm
10 inches = 25 cm
12 inches = 30 cm
20 inches = 50 cm

Volume (Dry) Measurements

¼ teaspoon = 1 milliliter
½ teaspoon = 2 milliliters
¾ teaspoon = 4 milliliters
1 teaspoon = 5 milliliters
1 tablespoon = 15 milliliters
¼ cup = 59 milliliters
⅓ cup = 79 milliliters
½ cup = 118 milliliters
⅔ cup = 158 milliliters
¾ cup = 177 milliliters
1 cup = 225 milliliters
4 cups or 1 quart = 1 liter
½ gallon = 2 liters
1 gallon = 4 liters

Volume (Liquid) Measurements

1 teaspoon = ⅙ fluid ounce = 5 milliliters
1 tablespoon = ½ fluid ounce = 15 milliliters
2 tablespoons = 1 fluid ounce = 30 milliliters
¼ cup = 2 fluid ounces = 60 milliliters
⅓ cup = 2⅔ fluid ounces = 79 milliliters
½ cup = 4 fluid ounces = 118 milliliters
1 cup or ½ pint = 8 fluid ounces = 250 milliliters
2 cups or 1 pint = 16 fluid ounces = 500 milliliters
4 cups or 1 quart = 32 fluid ounces = 1,000 milliliters
1 gallon = 4 liters

Oven Temperature Equivalents, Fahrenheit (F) and Celsius (C)

100°F = 38°C
200°F = 95°C
250°F = 120°C
300°F = 150°C
350°F = 180°C
400°F = 205°C
450°F = 230°C

Weight (Mass) Measurements

1 ounce = 30 grams
2 ounces = 55 grams
3 ounces = 85 grams
4 ounces = ¼ pound = 125 grams
8 ounces = ½ pound = 240 grams
12 ounces = ¾ pound = 375 grams
16 ounces = 1 pound = 454 grams

INGREDIENTS

LET'S TALK FOR a moment about what makes a cupcake tick.

FLOUR

You can't really make much of a cupcake without flour, so we recommend that you buy the best quality flours that you can. Experiment with different combinations for cupcakes of various textures and flavors, or with whole grains for healthier cupcakes with more fiber and nutrients.

ALL-PURPOSE FLOUR is the flour most often used for our cupcakes. Like the name says, it's a multi-use flour that results in light-textured, fluffy cupcakes with a nice crumb. It's not a nutrition superstar but you can up the fiber and nutrient content by substituting a little whole-grain flour in the recipes (see below). We like unbleached flour because of its creamy color—and because we believe that bleach is better off in one's hair, not one's cupcakes.

WHOLE WHEAT PASTRY FLOUR is an excellent way to add whole grain goodness to cupcakes. Unlike regular whole wheat flour, which can make cupcakes too heavy, whole wheat pastry flour has less gluten and is ground much finer, resulting in a tender, fine-crumbed cake. You can substitute up to half the unbleached flour in a recipe with whole wheat pastry with excellent results. As in "your cupcake eaters will never guess that you're feeding them a whole grain" results.

RICE, QUINOA, AND OTHER NON-WHEAT, NON-GLUTEN–CONTAINING FLOURS are not used extensively in this book but it's nothing personal. Generally, substituting ¼ cup of other flour out of every 1 cup of wheat flour works just fine. Using more means you'll get different—sometimes interesting, sometimes unpredictable—results. Some of our testers have had much success with quinoa flour in particular, but more often than not, successful wheat-free baking requires a blending of three or more flours. We're not experts regarding gluten-free baking but we love gluten-free people just the same, hence a little cupcake recipe on page 46.

FLOURS TO AVOID: Anything that says it's for making bread. Those kinds of flours have too much gluten and can result in heavy, too-chewy cupcakes. Regular whole wheat flour is also too heavy and coarse for cupcakes (but great in muffins; then again, this book isn't called *Muffins Take Over the World*, is it?). We generally don't mess with self-rising flour, but if you love it go ahead—just be sure to omit the baking soda and baking powder from the recipes.

SUGAR AND OTHER SWEETENERS

GRANULATED SUGAR: Most of our cupcake recipes use sugar, mostly because the flavor, consistency, low cost, and ease of use can't be beat when it comes to baking cupcakes. Where we say "sugar" we mean ordinary granulated sugar or evaporated cane juice interchangeably. In fact, any dry sweetener will do. We know, some of you might be thinking, "But I thought this was a health food baking book!" Well, sometimes it is, but when it

comes down to it, this is a book about decadent dessert, which shouldn't be every meal of the day. Just every other day. Luckily, in this day and age we have lots of great options for organic, vegan (no animal bone char used in the processing) natural sugar.

CONFECTIONERS' SUGAR, OR POWDERED SUGAR as it's known in some circles, is essential for making fluffy buttercream frosting. Rejoice in knowing that there are many great organic and vegan varieties of powdered sugar hitting the shelves every day. You can make your own by whirring granulated sugar in a food processor or blender till powdery. If you're going to use it to make frosting, we recommend adding 1 teaspoon of cornstarch per cup of granulated sugar, as it will help thicken the final consistency of the frosting or icing.

SUPERFINE OR CASTOR SUGAR is just granulated sugar with a smaller grain that dissolves faster. Make it yourself like powdered sugar; just don't blend it as much.

BROWN SUGAR is just granulated sugar with a little molasses blended in. We like to use it in our autumny and outdoorsy recipes.

MAPLE SYRUP works great in baking. Reduce the amount of other liquids in a recipe accordingly if maple syrup is substituted for granulated sugar. We don't rely much on it for sweetening our cupcakes because it's expensive, yet it does make an appearance in a few recipes and toppings for its special flavor and texture.

RICE SYRUP is a tasty, natural sweetener made from brown rice. It has all kinds of health benefits that are too boring to mention here. All you need to know is that it tastes good. It can be difficult to bake with, so it's featured primarily in caramel-like toppings for cupcakes.

AGAVE NECTAR is a magical liquid sweetener made from the cactuslike plant that's also used to make tequila. With the consistency of honey, more sweetness than sugar, and a hint of buttery flavor, it can be substituted for sugar in recipes, with adjustments made to other liquids in the recipe. Generally, ¾ cup of agave nectar equals one cup of sugar in sweetness, along with reducing the total liquid by one-third to account for the additional liquid content from the nectar. Agave is also very expensive and therefore the natural sweetener of millionaires, so we don't use it very often in baking. Instead we feature it in some sublime toppings and frosting where its flavor and texture really shine. We prefer the taste of light agave nectar although light and dark can be used interchangeably.

OILS, MARGARINE, AND SHORTENINGS

CANOLA OIL: Canola is the fat of choice in our baking. It's healthy, cheap, and the neutral flavor works with any kind of cupcake you can imagine. Do your best to use organic canola oil to ensure that it is free of GMOs* Sunflower, safflower or vegetable oil will make a good substitute if canola isn't available, but stay away from strongly flavored oils like peanut or olive.

MARGARINE: When used in frostings, margarine gives a nice, buttery flavor and a good mouthfeel. We don't bake with it too often because if overcreamed with the sugar, it can lead to sinking cupcakes. But every once in a while we break out the Old Marge for some totally faux buttery, tender cupcakes. And, of course, we only endorse trans-fat free, dairy-free varieties because we want you to live a long, healthy life abundant with cupcake making.

---

* GMOs are Genetically Modified Organisms, and unfortunately a large percentage of rapeseed fields, which is the plant that canola oil comes from, have fallen victim to genetic modification. We don't like it. We'll take our oils sans science fiction movie corporate control, thank you very much.

SHORTENING: Today's shortening ain't your mother's shortening. Now it's possible to get all-natural, nonhydrogenated, and even organic vegetable shortenings, some in convenient stick form that's easy to measure and use. We use it primarily in vegan buttercream frostings when a less obtrusive flavor than margarine is desired. It also makes frosting very stable at warmer temperatures and that is ideal for piping out decorations. However, we don't love shortening for baking cupcakes as it can make the finished cake oily, heavy, or bland.

COCONUT OIL, NON-HYDROGENATED AND REFINED: It's not as bad for you as you think! Long-suffering coconut oil is making a comeback in a big way after a few decades of bad press. As long as it's of the nonhydrogenated variety (found in natural food stores) it's a healthy fat in small amounts. We recommend using refined oil since the unrefined has a very strong coconut taste and aroma, which is fine if all you ever intend to bake is coconut cupcakes with coconut frosting.

SOY MILK, RICE MILK, OTHER "MILKS," AND YOGURTS

Plain old **SOY MILK** plays a big role in these cupcakes, providing the main source of liquid. Buttermilk—which provides leavening properties and a tender crumb in non-vegan cakes—is easily done up vegan style by whisking soy milk with a little vinegar and allowing to curdle for a minute or two (see Apple Cider Vinegar). Most of our recipes were developed with soy milk, but rice milk can be substituted too. **RICE MILK** won't curdle quite like soy milk but will get the job done, plus it has a milder flavor and can create lighter-textured cupcakes.

COCONUT MILK AND NUT MILKS: Coconut milk makes for exceptionally moist and flavorful cupcakes. We use regular and reduced-fat coconut milk interchangeably, so you can choose your battle. Almond and hazelnut milks work well in cupcakes that contain those respective nuts.

SOY AND RICE YOGURT: We adore soy yogurt in baking and it helps make some really light, fluffy, and moist cupcakes. Rice yogurt will pretty much do the same thing. We alternate between using plain and vanilla soy yogurts as the mood strikes us.

APPLE CIDER VINEGAR

You'll probably wonder why we put this in everything (see Soy Milk: something about curdles). Along with that stuff, vinegar helps the cupcakes rise and promotes a tender crumb. Use regular old white vinegar or brown rice vinegar if apple cider vinegar isn't available.

FLAVOR EXTRACTS

Get yourself a great big bottle of the best vanilla extract you can afford. Since vegan cupcakes don't have all the pesky butter and eggs that can overpower the flavor of baked goods, you'll be able to really taste the vanilla and other extracts you add. Avoid artificial flavors, particularly non-fruit ones like vanilla, chocolate, or coffee, since science can't solve every problem. In addition to vanilla, get a good-sized bottle of almond extract, as almond complements chocolate and other flavors so perfectly, you'll want to use it a lot. It's possible to get so many other great flavor extracts: strawberry, caramel (check ingredients for vegan-ness), coffee, banana, and more. Some organic brands are even sweetened with precious agave. Collect a bunch and soon you'll be known as "That Magical Extract Lady (or Man)" and the local children will follow you wherever you go.

BAKING POWDER AND BAKING SODA

We use any brand of baking powder that is aluminum-free. As for baking soda, we make sure not to use the same box that absorbs the odors in the fridge.

COCOA POWDER AND CHOCOLATE

We sometimes call for Dutch-processed cocoa powder. It is lower in acidity than normal cocoa powder and has a more intense taste. Often you will hear that you need to adjust the amount of baking soda and baking powder in your recipes depending on the kind of cocoa powder you use, and it is scientifically correct, but God's honest truth is you can substitute one for the other in our recipes without making any other adjustments and your cupcakes will be none the wiser.

AGAR AGAR POWDER OR FLAKES

For adding a gelatinlike stability, firmness, and thickening to fillings, we use agar agar, a natural seaweed used in many Asian cuisines. It can be found in natural food, gourmet, and Asian groceries. We use either flake or powder form, dissolved in a liquid and heated to form a gel (it also comes in bar form, but it's annoying to measure and use for the purpose of cupcakes). The trick to using agar is allowing the agar mixture to come to a full boil in order to dissolve completely in the liquid, otherwise the mixture won't firm up properly. Powdered agar is easier to use as it dissolves in less than a minute; flakes need to soak in liquid prior to cooking, to be boiled for minutes longer and stirred to make sure all the flakes are dissolved.

Agar can also be incorporated into batters; boil it to dissolve with soy milk or juice before adding to other ingredients. It gives cupcakes a moist, soft crumb and shiny tops.

ARROWROOT POWDER, CORNSTARCH AND FRIENDS

You'll see frequent use of starches like arrowroot powder and cornstarch. We could tell you how arrowroot comes from the root of a tropical vine, but do you really need to know that? What should interest you instead is that arrowroot is an excellent thickener that, when cooked, makes crystal clear sauces and creamy, custardlike fillings without the annoying addition of eggs. It needs to be mixed with a cold liquid before heating, and when it is fully cooked it will turn from a cloudy liquid to clear and thicken very quickly, so be sure to stir constantly!

Cornstarch does pretty much the same thing and can be interchanged with arrowroot in most recipes, but it doesn't cook up as fine or clear in a sauce. We like to sift a little cornstarch, too, into some cupcake batters to create soft, tender and extra "cakey" cupcakes.

Tapioca is another starch made from a tropical root and is used much like arrowroot. It has even more super gelling properties than other starches, so a little goes a long way.

ORDERING INGREDIENTS ONLINE

We tried to be as practical as possible in most of our ingredient lists but sometimes buying online from exotic and enchanting lands (like Newark) might be necessary for a recipe or two. If you can't find an ingredient at your local natural food market, the Internet is here to help.

Bob's Red Mill

www.bobsredmill.com

You can usually find Bob's flours, sugars, and flaxseeds in a health food store (and increasingly, in many supermarkets) but he also makes himself available to you online. Bob has everything a baker desires, and he's cute, too.

Food Fight! Vegan Grocery

www.foodfightgrocery.com

Get your Suzanne's Ricemellow Creme, cute candies for decorating, vegan whipped cream that actually tastes good, and vegan sprinkles.

Economy Candy

www.economycandy.com

This is where we get our chocolate lentils (they are sort of like that other chocolate candy with a colorful candy shell). Economy doesn't list product ingredients on their Web site but they have confirmed that they are vegan; if you don't believe me, then e-mail them.

Baker's Catalogue

www.bakerscatalogue.com

Fancy flours, baking gadgets galore, and deep, dark, black cocoa powder made by King Arthur himself!

Pangea Vegan Store

www.veganstore.com

Get your soy milk powder here, plus the Pangea Store's very own brand of vegan white chocolate chips!

TOOLS FOR TAKING OVER THE WORLD

JUST AS NASA has their tools for exploring space, we have ours for baking cupcakes and they are just as important. Maybe if Galileo had focused his attention on baking instead of telescopes, cupcakes would have been discovered a few centuries earlier. No matter; we have the knowledge now.

FOR BAKING

Muffin pans

We suggest using shiny, aluminum muffin pans, as they produce the most consistently perfect results. The other options we don't like so much, and here's why:

❖ The metal pans of the darker, coated variety result in cupcakes with rougher, chewier sides. That may be okay for muffins but for our cupcakes we want softness and tenderness.

❖ The silicon muffin pans that are so popular with the kids these days can wreak havoc on your cupcakes. Sure, nothing sticks to these pans and they come in pretty colors. But we noticed problems ranging from soggy, crumbly cupcakes to unevenly baked and inconsistent cupcakes, and worst of all, cupcakes whose tops just plain fell right off. Again, silicon pans may work for muffins, but cupcakes are more delicate and need pampering.

❖ The disposable muffin pans we will reluctantly let you use. We didn't notice too much of a difference in cupcake quality, but because of their disposable nature we can't really endorse them wholeheartedly.

Mixing bowls

You'll need two nice-sized, medium mixing bowls. What do we mean by nice-sized? You should have at least five inches of space left over after adding all the ingredients, because you want plenty of space while mixing the batter. We use glass, plastic, and metal bowls that have perfectly round insides for easy, consistent mixing. Ideally, mixing bowls will not be plastic because plastic absorbs weird odors, but really, who cares?

Most of our recipes call for two bowls, one for the dry ingredients and one for the wet (note that more often than not we include the sugar with the wet ingredients). In most cases we sift the dry ingredients into the wet, so use the bigger of your mixing bowls for wet ingredients.

Smaller mixing bowl

A smaller bowl is convenient for mixing frostings. We wouldn't call it a *small* bowl, just smaller. To describe the size: imagine someone eating a bowl of cereal that is big but not so ridiculously big you feel a need to laugh and point. So yeah, a little bigger than average.

Sifter

Sifting is a necessary part of cupcake baking because it aerates the flour, making it lighter and more manageable. It also ensures that there are no clumps of baking soda or chocolate in your batter. Our favorite sifter is actually a fine mesh strainer (or sieve), preferably with a long handle and rounded hooks on the opposite end for resting on the bowl. You can also

use a proper sifter, which looks like a big metal German beer stein and has either a hand crank or a device on the handle that you press to crank. We prefer the fine mesh strainer—easier to clean, and sometimes we just place it on top of the wet ingredient mixing bowl and sift the ingredients right into the batter.

Rubber spatula

Rubber spatulas are useful for making sure that you get every last bit of batter. A fancy heatproof silicon one is also nice to have when making ganache or cooked toppings.

Wire whisk

A wire whisk whips wet ingredients into a frenzy. But a strong fork will work as well.

Large wooden spoon

Use a large wooden spoon for folding ingredients into the batter.

Electric handheld mixer

Handheld mixers are the easiest and most efficient tools for small batches of batter. They are also useful for mixing thick frostings to a fluffy consistency.

Microplane grater

For zesting citrus and freshly grating nutmeg.

Cooling rack

Baked stuff cools quicker and more evenly when set on a cooling rack. And without them the bottoms of cooling cupcakes can get soggy—so sad. There's no reason not to have them; they cost peanuts.

Oven thermometer

Why does one need an extra thermometer when there's one right on the oven? Because ovens are not to be trusted. They are your enemies, and an impartial oven thermometer prevents backstabbing. It's another cheap-o gadget that makes for happy bakers and happy cupcakes.

FOR DECORATING

Small metal frosting spatula

This is sometimes referred to as a palette knife but you don't need a full-sized one for your little munchkin cupcakes. They are great for spreading thick frostings into a smooth, swooping finish and they work much better than a thin butter knife.

Cake decorating sets

Most houseware stores and large supermarkets carry cake decorating sets. It's usually a few plastic pastry bags and four to six decorating tips, plus some food coloring that we usually discard. These sets will get the job done just fine, but when you are ready to get all serious and brain surgeon about your cupcake decorating, you can stop in at either a baking or kitchen supply store and choose other tips to experiment with.

Pastry bags

Have on hand several disposable, plastic pastry bags. In a super punk-rock pinch you can stuff frosting into zip-top bags, seal the top, and cut a tiny hole in one of the bottom corners. It's a little messy and unpredictable, but that's anarchy for you. If you find that you love decorating so much, it's worth it to procure a cloth pastry bag; this will make you feel very professional and has the added benefit of being reusable so it's better for the environment and you will always have one when you need it.

Decorating tips

Decorating tips are standardized by number to make life easier for us homemakers. For cupcake decorating we stick pretty closely to three types of tips. Yeah, we're all kinds of crafty but we don't have the patience for intensive decorating, especially when equally awesome results can be had with a few flicks of the wrist and some creative garnish placement. We use the star tip (#21) for swirling frosting into a little mound of decorative heaven. You can also use it to make stars or cute star flowers. The writing tip (#3) is for, well, writing, but also for piping thin icing into squigglies, stripes, zig-zags and other Jackson Pollack-like decorations. Tip #104 is the rose tip. It's freaking crazy but if you have the patience then go for it.

Our other favorite tips are #809 and #827. These do not come in a kit and will most likely need to be procured at a kitchen supply or baking store. They are large, wide-mouthed decorating tips that are fun for applying mousse or buttercream into a luscious, swirly mountain of yum. Most kitchen supply stores have tips stocked in small bins in their decorating section, but sometimes they are kept in what must be a high security safe behind the counter and you have to ask an employee to get them for you.

Don't feel like you have to have those things or your cupcakes won't be pretty. We lived for years without any of this and still made cute cupcakes. If all you've got is the back of a spoon and a plastic bag with a hole cut out of the corner, so be it! Thousands have walked in your shoes before—be proud of your cupcake-making ancestry and hold your head high.

SEVEN RULES FOR RIGHTEOUS CUPCAKES

WHAT WOULD BE the opposite of the seven deadly (baking) sins? Well, that's what this list is. Follow these guidelines and you should always have perfect cuppers. If not, refer to the troubleshooting section, page 21.

1. Line your muffin pans immediately after preheating the oven. You want them ready and waiting when the batter is complete.

2. Use an ice cream scooper with a release mechanism for easy pouring and filling. It works perfectly because batter can't collect in any corners, plus you get consistent measurements each time you fill a liner.

3. Spray your batter-pouring implement with cooking spray before dipping it in the batter. This way the batter pours out gracefully.

4. Don't overfill the cupcake liner—two-thirds to three-quarters of the way full is perfect. They're going to rise and you don't want them to come out muffin shaped. (Or maybe you do, we don't know.)

5. When the cupcakes are done baking, remove them from the oven and let them cool in the pan for five to ten minutes. Then transfer them to a cooling rack to prevent sogginess.

6. Make sure that the cupcakes are fully cooled before filling or icing, unless otherwise indicated in a recipe. Spreading icing onto a still-warm cupcake is the work of fools.

7. If you don't have an oven thermometer, don't come crying to us.

TROUBLESHOOTING
When Bad Things Happen to Good Cupcakes

SOMETIMES IT SEEMS like no matter how many times you give your seat on the train to a pregnant lady, open doors for old people, or recycle, bad things still happen when you bake cupcakes. Below is a little go-to guide for just those times when things mysteriously don't work out. We don't have all the answers, but here are suggested solutions to some of the more common problems that happen with cupcakes.

EXHIBIT A: *My cupcakes sank!*

Suspect #1: Too cold oven/too hot oven/oven not preheated enough

Solution: Use an oven thermometer to ensure that your oven is the proper temperature for baking cupcakes. Most crappy old ovens (no, we're not bitter) need 15 to 20 minutes to get fully hot.

Suspect #2: Opening the oven door before it's time/removing cupcakes from oven prematurely

Solution: Don't peek! The first fifteen minutes of a cupcake's life is a critical time when most of the rising takes place and the structure sets, so even the tiniest draft or disturbance from an open oven door can cause a fall. However, the more sugar/moisture/fat a cupcake has, the longer the rising/setting time will be. So, don't remove cupcakes from the oven, even to test, until the minimum amount of time has passed. Master the art of testing a cupcake by opening the oven door carefully, yet quickly, dipping the toothpick into the nearest cupcake's center, and gently closing the oven door. A final tip: cupcakes are close to being done when you can smell that great cupcake fragrance wafting through your kitchen. By then it's usually okay to peek.

Suspect #3: Too much liquid/sugar/fat in batter
Solution: Some of these recipes require adding "premade" ingredients such as fruit preserves or soy yogurt, and different brands may have different moisture or sugar contents. Stir products to distribute any excess moisture before using, or in the case of soy yogurt, pour out any excess water that has collected. Experiment with different brands until the desired results are achieved. Of course you aren't on your own here; we will let you know if precautions should be taken in any given recipe.

Suspect #4: Overmixing
Solution: Overmixing can be a problem when creaming solid fats (like margarine) with sugar. Margarine can get too soft and melted from overbeating and lose valuable air bubbles that lift the cake's structure, hence the occasional problems when using margarine. The same goes for undermixing; all the ingredients must be evenly moistened and distributed to avoid rising prob-

lems. See Exhibit B for more information on the criminal history of overmixing.

EXHIBIT B: *Weird lumps and bumps! (Or, are these cupcakes hitting puberty?)*
Suspect #1: Overmixing (repeat offender)
Solution: Manhandling the batter can cause cupcakes to rise unevenly or form strange bumps and shapes. Use a light touch; often it's enough to just moisten ingredients and eliminate large lumps. As a rule, don't mix cupcake batter for more than one minute when using an electric mixer; you can go a little longer when mixing by hand. Overmixing can also lead to tunnels, "wormholes," and a tough, chewy cupcake, so don't do it!

Suspect #2: Cupcakes placed on a too-high oven rack
Solution: All cupcakes should be placed on a baking rack in the center of the oven. Arrange racks before preheating the oven, unless your hands are made out of asbestos.

Suspect #3: Oven temperature is too high or uneven
Solution: Again, the oven thermometer is your friend. Set it on the center rack for at

least 20 minutes, where the cupcakes will bake, for an accurate reading.

Suspect #4: Too many cupcakes in the oven
Solution: You may be in a hurry to bake fifty cupcakes for the band who's crashed on your living room floor, but some ovens don't take kindly to cramming in a lot of pans at once. If you to double or triple a recipe and bake them all at the same time, and the cupcakes are coming out funny-shaped or at different stages of doneness, you just might have to go back to baking one pan at a time. So tell that band to relax and change the cat litter for you instead, because a cupcake artiste! cannot be rushed. Don't panic, though; it is fine to double any of these recipes—just be warned that depending on your oven to bake them all together could be a pitfall.

EXHIBIT C: *My buttercream frosting looks curdled and nasty!*

Prime Suspect: Ingredients that are too cold/ingredients that are too warm
Solution: Make sure your margarine and shortening is at room temperature. Before you cream your solid fats with sugar, make sure they have been properly warmed to room temperature to avoid separated or lumpy frosting. Allow the margarine or shortening to sit on the kitchen counter for at least 15 to 20 minutes—as long as 30 minutes if the room is cool. Properly warmed margarine or shortening will have shiny, not greasy, appearance, and lightly pressing your finger on a wrapped bar will leave a slight indentation. Don't let it get too warm, however. If it looks too oily or is starting to melt, stick it back in the refrigerator for 10 minutes and check it again. If it's too warm, icing won't cream properly and could curdle as well.

While you're at it, make sure the rest of your ingredients are at room temperature, too. Not so much an issue with sugar, but don't throw ice-cold soy milk into a frosting either.

EXHIBIT D: *My frosting looked great in the bowl, but like gravy on the cupcake!*

Prime Suspect: You and your impatience
Solution: It could be that the cupcakes are still too warm to frost. The bottom and the sides, not just the top, should not have the slightest trace of warmth when applying frosting. A few of the glazes can take a warmer cupcake. It could also be that it's

just too damned hot everywhere, so holding off on vegan buttercream in the middle of August and opting for fresh peaches, instead, will save you some aggravation and a dozen greasy cupcakes.

EXHIBIT E: *My cupcakes didn't rise enough!*

See Exhibit A for possible suspects. Many of the reasons—oven not hot enough, uneven heating—are similar. But there are a few others like . . .

Suspect #1: Batter has been sitting around for too long
Solution: Use that batter pronto! The chemical reaction created by baking powder, baking soda, acidic ingredients, and trapped air generated by beating is powerful yet fleeting, so once the batter has been mixed and poured into the pan, put it in the preheated oven as soon as possible. You did preheat the oven, didn't you?

Suspect #2: Expired baking powder
Solution: Maybe it's been in the family for generations, but that baking powder in the old, beat-up can that's been in the cabinet since stirrup pants were cool has lost much of its reactivity over time. It just won't work

right. Buy a new can just for cupcakes, and while you're at it, drop off those acid wash jeans at the Goodwill on your way back from the store.

EXHIBIT F: *My cupcakes are stuck to the liner! (Or, letting-go issues)*

Suspect #1: Impatient you (repeat offender)
Solution: Go do a sudoku puzzle and relax. If you try to eat a cupcake before it cools we cannot be held responsible for what happens.

Suspect #2: Overbaking
Solution: Sometimes accidents happen; you misjudge the doneness of a cupcake and let it bake for too long. Other times you guess-timate the baking times. Get a kitchen timer and put your mind at ease.

If this gets to be a chronic problem, it may be solved by spraying the liners lightly with nonstick cooking spray before adding batter.

DECORATING YOUR CUPCAKES

I F WE COULD create a new dictionary entry for the word "fun," it would be solely composed of the joys of decorating cupcakes. Okay, it might include something about kittens and puppies and a few unmentionable activities, but cupcakes would take center stage.

As with lots of fun activities, the more you do it, the better your skills will get. When it comes to decorating, be adventurous with food colors, candy sprinkles, or piping on that frosting with a flourish of the wrist. Don't be afraid to get a little messy—remember, you are a cupcake artist immersed in your work! Just bribe somebody with cupcakes to clean up after you.

Most of the decorating instructions in this book require a few special tools. Be sure to read Tools for Taking Over the World (page 15) before checking out this chapter.

HOW TO PIPE VEGAN BUTTERCREAM FROSTING

Buttercream frosting is what most people think of when it comes to decorating, eating, and gazing admiringly at cupcakes. And who are we to argue: its smooth, fluffy texture and the ease of tinting it to almost any shade makes it perfect not just for slathering on top of cupcakes, but also for creating snazzy additions like flowers, stars, and lettering. Here are a few tips to keep in mind when working with VEGAN FLUFFY BUTTERCREAM FROSTING (page 142).

BEFORE YOU START DECORATING: When using more than one frosting flavor or color, or even just a lot of one kind of frosting, prepare all the recipes and fill pastry bags before you begin decorating. It's annoying to break your decorating flow to stop and prepare another bag or batch of frosting. If you're planning to use different tips for different shapes on the same cupcake, consider using a screw-on nozzle set with your pastry bags.

FILLING A PASTRY BAG: Fit the pastry bag with the tip of your choice. Next, cuff the end of the pastry bag, like how your mom used to cuff the bottoms of your pants. The cuff should be about 3 inches. The purpose of this is multifold; to make sure that you don't overfill the bag, to get as much frosting as close to the nozzle as possible, and to avoid getting frosting on the sides of the bag where it could end up squirting out of the top. Use a rubber spatula to handle frosting and fill pastry bags. Scoop frosting into the bag, carefully shake the bag a little to get rid of any air bubbles, and gently squeeze the top of the bag to push the frosting to the bottom. (It's a good idea to set the bag

above the frosting bowl so that any excess frosting pushed through the nozzle lands back in the bowl.) It's also easier to control a pastry bag that hasn't been filled more than two-thirds of the way. Uncuff the bag and either twist it or tie it shut with a rubberband. Squeeze the bag a little more before you're ready to decorate, to eliminate any last little air bubbles and to "test" the tip to make sure it's creating the kind of results you're after.

THE RIGHT TEMPERATURE FOR THE RIGHT JOB: When preparing flowers, stars, or any detailed piped-on decoration, keep prepared buttercream frosting chilled until ready to use. Conversely, buttercream or mousse that is going to be spread on the cupcake with a knife or piped on with a very large nozzle should be allowed to sit at room temperature for about 10 minutes, especially if it's very firm when first removed from the refrigerator. Spreading on too-firm frosting can tear delicate cupcake tops. Finally, if your frosting starts to look greasy or less fluffy, it's getting too warm to work with. Pop the whole thing, bags and bowl and all, in the fridge to cool and firm up.

FOR A PRETTY MARBLED EFFECT WITH PIPED FROSTING: Load up a pastry bag with half vanilla buttercream frosting and half chocolate frosting. Or try tinting one-third to one-half of a batch of vanilla buttercream with food coloring and a contrasting flavor extract (check out the pink and white frosting for the PISTACHIO ROSEWATER CUPPERS on page 117). Be sure to tap the bag and squeeze out any air bubbles to ensure smooth delivery of frosting.

EASY CLEANING: An easier way to clean off greasy buttercream from pastry bags, tips, and mixing bowls: Fill the used mixing bowl with hot water and a squirt of dishwashing liquid. Agitate the water and get everything sudsy, then toss in the bags and tips. Allow to soak for a few minutes, slosh everything around a little more, and clean with a sponge. The hot water and soap will help melt off and emulsify the fats. Rinse one more time with hot water and dry.

ADVANCED PIPING: Here's where we tell you to leave the nest. Most pastry bag and decorator tip kits come with a little pamphlet that instructs in the making of roses, leaves, etc., and can be a great place to start learning more advanced decorating tricks. Check out some in-depth decorating books and Web sites if you're serious about making frosting flowers and details beyond plopping out pointy little shapes with a star tip. However, we still love you even if you don't feel this desire stirring inside. Your cupcakes can still taste awesome and look cute, no matter if you ever top them with orchids made out of chocolate ganache.

STENCIL DECORATING

This is the arts and crafts part of *Vegan Cupcakes Take Over the World*. Make a paper stencil, sprinkle on the powdered sugar and spices, and people will think a reality show just walked in on your cupcakes and gave them a sassy makeover.

1. Measure out a square of sturdy construction-type paper; a 4 by 4-inch square should do. Flip over a cupcake liner and trace a circle that more or less is the circumference of the top of a cupcake. You'll want to have an extra inch or more around the circle.

2. Fold your square in half, then fold it in half again. With a sharp pair of scissors cut out a few shapes—hearts, diamonds, hearts, moons . . . oops,

whatever—but keep it relatively simple and the shapes a little bit exaggerated. Think first-grade art class snowflakes.

3. Unfold and get as flat as possible. If you have the time, set inside a large, heavy book to press out the creases. Your stencil is now ready for sprinkling! Just be sure you have enough room around the stencil to catch excess cocoa/spices and for something to hold on to. Stencil cupcakes on a sheet of newspaper or paper towels for quick clean up later.

4. Cheat this process by using a paper doily. Just be sure to get one with large-ish holes, as too-small or detailed shapes won't really come out when stenciled.

MAKING STUFF OUT OF MARZIPAN (FLOWERS, CRITTERS, ETC.)

We use marzipan almond candy dough to decorate the Green Tea Cupcakes (page 97) in this book, but really there's no reason you can't shape marzipan into little daisies, deer, daikons, or duck-billed platypi. It's all vegan as long as your marzipan doesn't contain egg albumin, so read that label before you buy! We've found lots of great marzipan in tubes and cans in the baking aisle of better supermarkets.

❖ To work with marzipan: have a clean surface and one or more of the following: food coloring, powdered sugar, waxed paper, a small, smooth rolling pin, cutting tools like a thin sharp knife, decorative fondant cutters in different shapes, and toothpicks for making fine imprints.

❖ Color marzipan by kneading it with a small amount of food coloring. Paste works best, but liquid works too. You'll have to knead for a few minutes to distribute the color evenly and avoid any marbled effect. Set aside tinted marzipan in an airtight container if not using immediately.

❖ Roll out the marzipan on a surface lightly dusted with confectioners' sugar and cut out shapes with fondant cutters (or small cookie cutters) or a knife. Rolling between two sheets of waxed paper is another way to do this. Try stacking different shapes of different colors on top of each other (like a star on a circle) for a different effect.

❖ Start shaping: it's just like the kind of clay you played with as a kid, so model away. Dust your work surface lightly with confectioners' sugar, and dip your finger in confectioners' sugar too if the marzipan gets too sticky. Place your finished shapes on wax paper, carefully cover and keep refrigerated until ready to use. Store marzipan in a sealed container or tightly wrapped in plastic wrap to keep from drying out when not using.

CHOCOLATE SHAVINGS AND CURLS

Nothing beats a flourish of chocolate shavings or curls to instantly add some class to your cupcakes. The simplest method involves a good quality vegan dark chocolate bar and a sharp, clean vegetable peeler. Allow the chocolate bar to warm up to room temperature, and then run the vegetable peeler on the edge of the bar for tiny curls, or along the smooth underside of the bar for longer shavings. Save the curls on a dish or shred directly onto frosted cupcakes. Store shavings and curls in a cool place until ready to use.

For big curls, spread melted semisweet chocolate onto waxed paper with a spatula, making an oblong shape with as smooth a surface as you can manage. Allow chocolate to cool to room temperature until firm to touch. Run a large, sharp veggie peeler (or a sharp paring knife) lengthwise on the chocolate, taking care not to dig too deep, less than $1/8$ inch. Gently lift the curls onto a plate or onto cupcakes. This is a slightly trickier method worth mastering that can help you make really big, fat curls that look like they came from a fancy bakery.

MORE CUTE TOPPERS

We also like to keep decorating simple. Here's a quick list of cute things you may already have on hand that look great on top of cupcakes, beyond the usual sprinkles and chocolate jimmies, that broadcast to the world your veganitude.

Edibles
- ❖ Cinnamon Sticks
- ❖ Vegan gummies
- ❖ Gel fruit slices (usually vegan made with pectin, but check ingredients)
- ❖ Coffee lentils (check ingredients)

- Ground cinnamon or nutmeg
- Semisweet chocolate chips and vegan white chocolate chips
- Colorful, fun-shaped kid's vegan breakfast cereals
- Chopped chocolate-covered peanuts, hazelnuts, almonds, raisins
- Vegan gumdrops, licorice whips, jelly beans
- Crushed vegan cookies
- Fresh sliced strawberries, mangoes, cantaloupe, papaya, kiwis, star fruit, bananas
- Chocolate-covered pretzels, coarsely chopped
- Edible flowers (check the produce aisle for prepacked flowers sold as "edible." Don't use flowers from a florist, as they are often sprayed with chemicals. Or grow your own pansies or violets just for cupcakes!)

Non-edibles

. . . And a few non-edible items that just look too cute on cupcakes, to be removed by the cupcake eater before consuming. Not recommended for little kids or anyone who feels compelled to eat plastic or wood just because it's on top of a cupcake.

- Scrabble pieces (awesome for spelling out a name on birthday cupcakes)
- Small plastic farm animals, cats, lizards, frogs, unicorns
- Fake flowers (wash and dry before using)
- A single clove, sweet-looking on a gingerbread cupcake topped with a white icing
- Candles (We know you know not to eat these, but just in case you come from a planet that doesn't have birthdays.)

PART TWO

THE RECIPES

BASIC CUPCAKES

THESE ARE ALL-PURPOSE chocolate and vanilla cupcakes that you can use for just about anything your heart desires, and some for special cases. Your aunt is on a gluten-free diet? No problem (see page 46)! Your boyfriend is trying to shed a few pounds? Send him your way (see page 41)! Your third cousin once removed is a diabetic? See page 44. Makes no difference to you, because you have the cupcake prowess to handle any situation.

GOLDEN VANILLA CUPCAKES

MAKES 12 CUPCAKES

THIS MULTIPURPOSE, NO-NONSENSE cupcake should be in your holster opposite Your BASIC CHOCOLATE CUPCAKE (page 37) if you are considering the rough and tumble life of a cupcake gunslinger. And they're also nice for birthdays, bake sales, and baby showers.

We've included two options for these made with either canola oil or margarine, both resulting in slightly different but yummy cupcakes. Canola oil makes a never-fail cupcake with a light texture, great with any vanilla-based variation. Margarine can be a little trickier to work with, but the buttery flavor, golden color, and delicate texture it gives cupcakes are worth the effort. These are also a little less sweet than some other cupcakes and perfect for loading intense frostings like THICK CHOCO-LATE FUDGEY FROSTIN' (page 161), CHOCOLATE BUTTERCREAM (page 144) or RICH CHOCOLATE GANACHE TOPPING (page 143), or any variation of Vegan Fluffy Buttercream Frosting (page 142).

We've included a secret tip at the end for really golden cupcakes (see Sprinkles below). Try these for BROOKLYN VS. BOSTON CREAM PIE CAKES (page 65) or topped with ridiculously tall swirls of Vegan Fluffy Buttercream Frosting for the best birthday cupcakes ever.

INGREDIENTS

1 cup soy milk

1 teaspoon apple cider vinegar

1¼ cups all-purpose flour

2 tablespoons cornstarch

¾ teaspoon baking powder

½ teaspoon baking soda

¼ teaspoon salt (increase salt to
  ½ teaspoon if you're using oil
  instead of margarine)

½ cup non-hydrogenated margarine,
  softened, or ⅓ cup canola oil

¾ cup granulated sugar

2 teaspoons vanilla extract

¼ teaspoon almond extract, caramel
  extract, or more vanilla extract

DIRECTIONS

1. Preheat oven to 350°F and line muffin pan with cupcake liners.

2. Whisk the soy milk and vinegar in a measuring cup and set aside a few minutes to get good and curdled.

3. If using margarine: Sift the flour, cornstarch, baking powder, baking soda, and salt into a large bowl and mix.

4. In a separate large bowl, use a handheld mixer at medium speed to cream the margarine and sugar for about 2 minutes until light and fluffy, but don't beat past two minutes. Beat in the vanilla and other extract, if using, then alternate beating in the soy milk mixture and dry ingredients, stopping to scrap the sides of the bowl a few times.

5. If using oil: Beat together the soy milk mixture, oil, sugar, vanilla, and other extracts, if using, in a large bowl. Sift in the flour, cornstarch, baking powder, baking soda, and salt and mix until no large lumps remain.

6. Fill cupcake liners two-thirds of the way and bake for 20 to 22 minutes

till done. Transfer to a cooling rack and let cool completely before frosting.

Variations

REALLY GOLDEN CUPCAKES: In a small stainless-steel saucepan beat a generous pinch of turmeric powder into the soy milk. Stirring occasionally to prevent a skin from forming on the top, cook mixture over medium-low heat till soy milk just starts to simmer, about 2 to 3 minutes. When turmeric powder appears to be dissolved and the soy milk has a light yellow hue, remove from heat and cool for 5 minutes. Add vinegar and proceed as directed.

FLAVORED GOLDEN CUPCAKES: These simple cupcakes can go anywhere with a change of flavor extracts: add 1 to 1½ teaspoons your choice of coffee, coconut, or orange extract, or 1 teaspoon ground cinnamon or pumpkin pie spice. Spread tops with any topping, frosting, or filling you can imagine.

STRAWBERRY TALLCAKES: Prepare Golden Vanilla Cupcakes and cool. Combine 1½ cups thinly sliced fresh strawberries with 3 tablespoons maple syrup and set aside to

Golden Vanilla Cupcakes with Fluffy
Buttercream Frosting
Your Basic Chocolate Cupcake with
Chocolate Buttercream Frosting

macerate for at least 30 minutes. Prepare VEGAN FLUFFY BUTTERCREAM FROSTING (page 142), or use any vegan whipped topping or even softened vanilla soy ice cream if eating right away. Spoon out cupcake centers and set aside (as illustrated with TIRAMISŪ CUPCAKES page 119). Fill centers of cupcakes with about 2 tablespoons sliced berries and juice, top with a dollop (up to 2 tablespoons) of frosting or topping, then gently but firmly press on cut-out cake top. Pipe on more frosting, spoon on more strawberries. Place cupcakes on individual serving dishes and add final toppings when ready to serve. These are messy and need to be eaten with a spoon.

LEMONY VANILLA CUPCAKES: Add an additional 1½ teaspoons lemon extract and 1 tablespoon finely grated lemon zest. Frost with LEMON BUTTERCREAM (page 96).

MIX-INS VANILLA CUPCAKES: Quick and easy additions to stir into vanilla cupcake batter; try folding in ⅓ to ⅔ cup of the following to batter just before filling liners: Finely chopped chocolate-covered almonds or peanuts, currants, smashed peanut brittle, finely chopped vegan sesame halva candy, vegan chocolate chips, or white chocolate chips.

YOUR BASIC CHOCOLATE CUPCAKE

MAKES 12 CUPCAKES

THE NAME SAYS it all, a simple but perfect, tender, and all-around wonderful chocolate cupcake. Change the look, flavor, and even nationality (with COCONUT PECAN FUDGE FROSTING, page 147, for GERMAN CHOCOLATE CUPCAKES) by topping with any frosting, glaze, or filling you can imagine. This recipe is the basis for so many great chocolate cupcakes in this book. We've been even known to whip up an unadorned batch and serve with a glass of cold soy milk when the need for good, honest chocolate cake arises.

INGREDIENTS

- 1 cup soy milk
- 1 teaspoon apple cider vinegar
- ¾ cup granulated sugar
- ⅓ cup canola oil
- 1 teaspoon vanilla extract
- ½ teaspoon almond extract, chocolate extract, or more vanilla extract
- 1 cup all-purpose flour
- ⅓ cup cocoa powder, Dutch-processed or regular
- ¾ teaspoon baking soda
- ½ teaspoon baking powder
- ¼ teaspoon salt

DIRECTIONS

1. Preheat oven to 350°F and line muffin pan with paper or foil liners.
2. Whisk together the soy milk and vinegar in a large bowl, and set aside for a few minutes to curdle. Add the sugar, oil, and vanilla extract, and other extract, if using, to the soy milk mixture and beat till foamy. In a separate bowl, sift together the flour, cocoa powder, baking soda, baking powder, and salt. Add in two batches to wet ingredients and beat till no large lumps remain (a few tiny lumps are okay).

3. Pour into liners, filling three-quarters of the way. Bake 18 to 20 minutes, until a toothpick inserted into the center comes out clean. Transfer to cooling rack and let cool completely.

Variations

PEANUT BUTTER CHOCOLATE HEAVENCAKES: Fill with Peanut Buttercream Frosting or Filling (page 151), and top with Rich Chocolate Ganache Topping (page 143). Pipe a cute swirl of remaining frosting on top of glazed cupcakes.

PEANUT BUTTER BOMBES: Double the Peanut Buttercream Filling or Frosting recipe (page 151) and frost into high, rounded domes on top of cupcakes. Chill till very firm, then carefully dribble with RICH CHOCOLATE GANACHE TOPPING (page 143). Decorate with chocolate shavings or curls or sprinkles.

CHOCOLATE MOCHA CUPCAKES: Add 2 tablespoons instant espresso or coffee to batter. Frost with VEGAN FLUFFY BUTTERCREAM FROSTING (page 142), replacing the soy milk in the frosting recipe with cold, strong coffee. Dust tops lightly with ground cinnamon or nutmeg.

GERMAN CHOCOLATE CUPCAKES: Like the lady said, frost generously with Coconut Pecan Fudge Frosting (page 147).

CHOCOLATE ORANGE CUPCAKES: Add 1½ teaspoons orange extract, or 1 tablespoon finely grated orange peel, or 2 tablespoons finely chopped candied orange peel, to cupcake batter. You can also replace up to ¼ cup of the liquid with orange liqueur in addition to any of the orange-y options. Frost with ORANGE BUTTERCREAM (page 145), adding 1 teaspoon orange extract to the buttercream in addition to the vanilla extract. Decorate tops of frosted cakes with a sliver of orange peel or orange candy sprinkles.

Sprinkles

Use Dutch-processed cocoa for darker cupcakes. Worth the effort to get, try these with a mixture of black cocoa powder (see ingredients section, page 12) and regular cocoa powder, for the deepest, darkest, and most ridiculously chocolatey chocolate cupcakes ever.

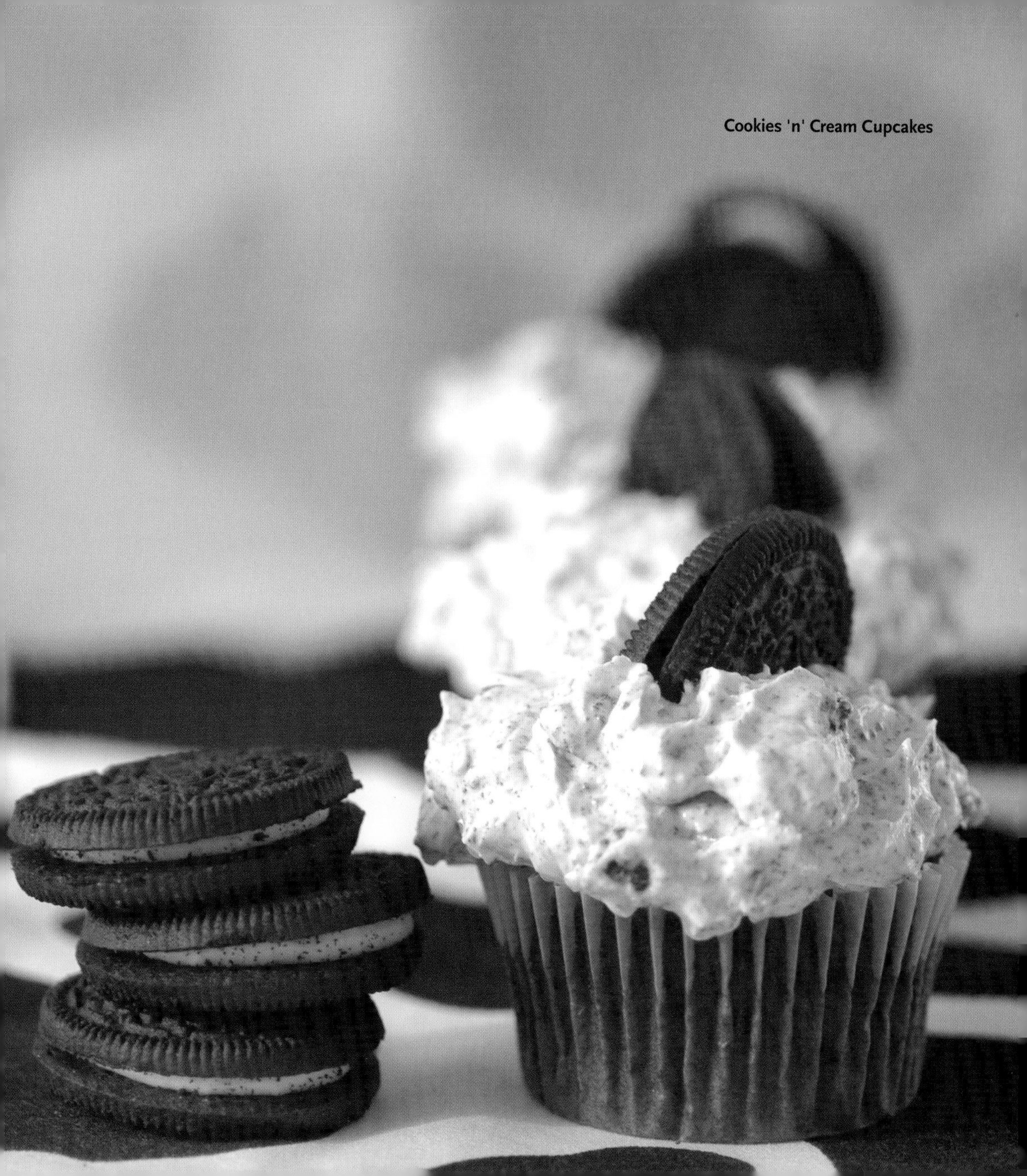

Cookies 'n' Cream Cupcakes

COOKIES 'N' CREAM CUPCAKES (PICTURED ON PAGE 39): Mix into cupcake batter 1 cup (about 10 cookies; chop first then measure) of coarsely chopped vegan chocolate cream-filled sandwich cookies (like Newman-O's). Bake as directed. Prepare VEGAN FLUFFY BUTTERCREAM FROSTING (page 142), and stir into frosting ½ cup finely mashed sandwich cookie crumbs. Frost cupcakes generously, and top each cupcake with half of a sandwich cookie.

FLAVOR EXTRACTS AND LIQUORS: Replace almond extract with 1 to 2 teaspoons of coconut, caramel, or raspberry extract. Also try adding up to 1 tablespoon of liquor such as rum, brandy, whiskey, or fruit cognac.

CHOCOLATE GINGER: Sift 2 teaspoons ground ginger into the flour. Fold in ⅓ cup chopped crystallized ginger to the batter. Top with RICH CHOCOLATE GANACHE (page 143). Place a piece of crystallized ginger in the center of the ganache before it sets.

SEXY LOW-FAT VANILLA CUPCAKES
with *Fresh Berries*

MAKES 12 CUPCAKES

YOU MIGHT THINK there's no way you could possibly get any sexier with all the cupcake baking you've been up to by now, but sometimes you just need to fit into that particular pair of pants (or skirt or dress or tube top) that makes you feel sexy . . . but you're not willing to give up cupcakes. Correction, there's no way in freakin' hell you're putting down those cupcakes. Now you don't have to, thanks to these vanilla-scented gems.

INGREDIENTS
For the cupcakes:
- ½ cup vanilla soy yogurt
- ⅔ cup vanilla or plain soy milk
- ¼ cup applesauce
- 3 tablespoons canola oil
- ¾ cup granulated sugar
- 1½ teaspoons vanilla extract
- 1¼ cup all-purpose flour
- 2 tablespoons cornstarch
- ¾ teaspoon baking powder
- ½ teaspoon baking soda
- ¼ teaspoon salt

For the Skinny Confectioners' Icing:
- 1 cup confectioners' sugar, sifted
- 1 to 3 teaspoons of soy milk or 1 tablespoon flavored syrup (like the kind used for flavoring lattes and Italian sodas)
- ½ cup seedless, smooth spreadable fruit or other preserves
- 1 cup fresh fruit or berries, washed, patted dry and thinly sliced if necessary

DIRECTIONS
TO MAKE THE CUPCAKES:

1. Preheat oven to 350°F and line a muffin pan with cupcake liners.
2. In a large bowl, whisk together yogurt, soy milk, applesauce, oil, sugar, and vanilla. Sift in flour, cornstarch, baking powder, baking soda, and salt, and mix.

**Sexy Low-Fat Vanilla Cupcakes
with Fresh Berries**

3. Fill cupcake liners three-quarters full. Bake 22 to 24 minutes until a knife or toothpick inserted through the center of one comes out clean. Transfer to a cooling rack to cool completely.

TO MAKE THE ICING:

1. Mix confectioners' sugar with soy milk or syrup, either with a fork or a small whisk. Mixture will resemble a very thick paste or batter. Carefully dribble in remaining soy milk, one teaspoon at a time, till mixture resembles a thin cake batter, adjusting additional soy milk by either less or more teaspoons till desired consistency is reached. If too watery, add in more confectioners' sugar by the tablespoon.

TO ASSEMBLE:

1. Spread top of cupcake with a few thin layers of spreadable fruit at room temperature. Neatly and evenly spread the layers for the most attractive appearance. Spoon a small circle of Skinny Confectioners' Icing on top of jam, decorate with fresh fruit, and carefully drizzle tops of berries with more icing.

✳ *Sprinkles* ✳

✦ We think fresh raspberries make everything taste awesome and their being naturally low-fat we feature them here, but any succulent, seasonal fruit will be fabulous. These tender yet firm cupcakes can support all the peaches, strawberries, blackberries, blueberries, mangoes, etc. you can top them with. The Skinny Confectioners' Icing is optional but adds an elegant, sweet garnish. Experiment with different preserves to mix and match with any fruit combination that tickles your fancy.

✦ Our dedicated vegan weight loss task force recommends making these with low-fat or even fat-free soy milk to streamline these cupcakes' fat and calorie profile.

SIMPLE VANILLA AND AGAVE NECTAR CUPCAKES

MAKES 12 CUPCAKES

AGAVE NECTAR (see Ingredients, page 10) makes an exceptionally fluffy and tender cupcake, with a deep golden hue. Agave sweetness is different from regular sugar . . . it's light and subtle, with a delectable buttery flavor and faintly flowery aroma. The slightly lower cooking time helps here because agave baked goods brown darker and faster than stuff made with sugar, so be sure to check that oven thermometer!

This is a very basic recipe to be play with; mix and match flavored extracts, mix-ins, and toppings. We especially like these spread thickly with THICK CHOCOLATE FUDGEY FROSTIN' (page 161), a thin layer of SUPER NATURAL AGAVE ICING (page 149), or a swirl of NOT-TOO-SWEET BLUEBERRY MOUSSE (page 153).

INGREDIENTS
- ⅔ cup soy milk
- ½ teaspoon apple cider vinegar
- ⅔ cup light agave nectar
- ⅓ cup canola oil
- 1½ teaspoon vanilla extract
- ½ teaspoon almond extract
- 1⅓ cups all-purpose flour
- ¾ teaspoon baking powder
- ½ teaspoon baking soda
- ¼ teaspoon salt

DIRECTIONS
1. Line muffin pan with cupcake liners and preheat oven to 325°F.
2. Mix the soy milk and apple cider vinegar in a large bowl; allow to sit for a few minutes to curdle. Beat in agave, oil, vanilla, and almond extract. Sift in the flour, baking powder, baking soda, and salt and mix until smooth. Fill liners two-thirds full. Bake 20 to 22 minutes until a knife or toothpick inserted into the center of a cupcake comes

out clean; don't overbake or cupcakes will be dry.

3. These cupcakes need to cool at least an hour before topping or filling, and also to develop the flavor and texture properly.

Variation

CHOCOLATE AGAVE CUPCAKES: Decrease flour to 1 cup, and sift in ⅓ cup cocoa powder along with the dry ingredients. If desired add one or more of the following: 2 tablespoons espresso powder, 1 teaspoon chocolate extract, or teaspoon orange extract. Try using dark agave nectar in this chocolate variation!

Sprinkles

We know we complained about agave being pricey and all, but it's worth the splurge for these special cupcakes. While no one in their right mind would ever take medical advice from us, many people with sugar sensitivities have had much success with agave-sweetened baked goods.

VANILLA GLUTEN FREEDOM CUPCAKES

MAKES 12 CUPCAKES

WE ALWAYS FEEL a kinship with gluten-free folks because they are as much of a pain in the butt when ordering food at a restaurant as a vegan is. Just because you can't have gluten doesn't mean you should be left out of the fun, and even if you *can* have gluten you might want to take a break from it every now and then to go easier on your tummy. We like how these taste, too. All the different textures of the flour make for a great mouth-feel and a nice spongy crumb. We give you the option of corn flour or almond meal because we tried both and couldn't tell which we liked better. Corn flour is finer than corn meal however, so make sure you get the right one when you are doing your shopping.

INGREDIENTS

1 cup soy milk
⅓ cup canola oil
¾ cup sugar
2 teaspoons vanilla extract
¼ teaspoon almond extract
¼ cup tapioca flour
2 tablespoons ground flax seed
⅓ cup corn flour or ⅓ cup almond flour
½ cup white rice flour
½ cup quinoa flour
1 teaspoon baking powder
½ teaspoon baking soda
¼ teaspoon salt

DIRECTIONS

1. Preheat oven to 350°F and line muffin tray with cupcake liners.
2. In a large mixing bowl combine soy milk, canola oil, sugar and extracts. Mix with an electric mixer on medium speed just to combine. Add tapioca flour and flax seed and mix vigorously for about a minute, until the tapioca flour is dissolved and the mixture is well emulsified.

3. Add the corn flour, white rice flour, quinoa flour, baking powder, baking soda and salt. Mix on medium-high for about 2 minutes. It's important to mix really well and you don't have to worry about over-mixing because, hey, there's no gluten!

4. Fill cupcake liners a little over three-quarters full, these won't rise as much as traditional cupcakes so you can fill them a little more than usual.

5. Bake for 20 to 23 minutes, until a toothpick or knife inserted through the center comes out clean. Transfer to a cooling rack and let cool completely before frosting.

CHOCOLATE GLUTEN FREEDOM CUPCAKES

MAKES 12 CUPCAKES

NOW FREEDOM COMES in chocolate as well!

INGREDIENTS

  1 cup soy milk
  ⅓ cup canola oil
  ¾ cup sugar
  2 teaspoons vanilla extract
  ¼ teaspoon almond extract
  ¼ cup tapioca flour
  2 tablespoons ground flax seed
  ⅓ cup unsweetened cocoa powder
  ½ cup white rice flour
  ½ cup quinoa flour
  1 teaspoon baking powder
  ½ teaspoon baking soda
  ¼ teaspoon salt

DIRECTIONS

1. Preheat oven to 350°F and line muffin tray with cupcake liners.

2. In a large mixing bowl combine soy milk, canola oil, sugar and extracts. Mix with an electric mixer on medium speed just to combine. Add tapioca flour and flax seed and mix vigorously for about a minute, until the tapioca flour is dissolved and the mixture is well emulsified.

3. Add the cocoa powder, white rice flour, quinoa flour, baking powder, baking soda and salt. Mix on medium-high for about 2 minutes. It's important to mix really well and you don't have to worry about over-mixing because, hey, there's no gluten!

4. Fill cupcake liners a little over three-quarters full, these won't rise as much as traditional cupcakes so you can fill them a little more than usual.

5. Bake for 20 to 23 minutes, until a toothpick or knife inserted through the center comes out clean. Transfer to a cooling rack and let cool completely before frosting.

CLASSIC CUPCAKES

THESE CUPCAKES ARE always in style, be they as simple as carrot cake or as sophisticated as a golden cupcake busting with vanilla custard. Great for any occasion or no special reason in particular, anyone would be thrilled and delighted to receive a dozen.

CARROT CAKE CUPCAKES
with *Cream Cheese Frosting*

MAKES 12 CUPCAKES

THESE DENSE, MOIST cupcakes pack in 29.3 percent more carrots, raisins, and nuts, per square centimeter than the leading vegan carrot cupcake. An engineering miracle when topped with VEGAN CREAM CHEESE FROSTING **(page 158), not to mention yummy.**

INGREDIENTS

⅔ cup all-purpose flour
¾ teaspoon baking soda
¼ teaspoon baking powder
¼ teaspoon salt
¼ teaspoon ground cinnamon
¼ teaspoon ground ginger
⅔ cup sugar
⅓ cup vegetable oil
⅓ cup soy yogurt (plain or vanilla)
1 teaspoon vanilla
1 cup finely grated carrots
¼ cup chopped walnuts
¼ cup raisins

For Decorating
⅓ cup chopped walnuts
1 recipe VEGAN CREAM CHEESE FROSTING,
    page 158

DIRECTIONS

1. Preheat oven to 350°F. Line muffin tin with 12 cupcake liners.

2. In a medium mixing bowl, mix together sugar, vegetable oil, yogurt and vanilla. Sift in the dry ingredients (flour, baking soda, baking powder, salt, spices) and mix until smooth. Fold in carrots, walnuts and raisins.

3. Spray the cupcake liners with non-stick baking spray. Fill the liners two-thirds full. Bake for 26 to 28 minutes, until a toothpick inserted through the center of one comes out clean.

4. Once fully cooled, top generously with cream cheese frosting.

Place chopped walnuts on a plate, then roll the edges of the cupcake in the chopped walnut. A raisin in the center is a cute garnish, or if serving immediately sprinkle finely grated carrot in the center.

GINGERBREAD CUPCAKES
with *Lemony Frosting*

MAKES 12 CUPCAKES

NOTHING SAYS WAITING for the holiday season to end like these moist, fluffy gingerbread cupcakes. Bring them to your next familial bash and eat them as you grit your teeth and marvel at your family. Top with LEMONY CREAM CHEESE FROSTING **(page 158)** or LEMONY BUTTERCREAM **(page 96).**

INGREDIENTS
1¼ cups all-purpose flour
1 teaspoon baking powder
½ teaspoon baking soda
3 teaspoons ground ginger
1 teaspoon ground cinnamon
¼ teaspoon ground cloves
¼ teaspoon salt
½ cup vegetable oil
⅓ cup light molasses
½ cup maple syrup
¼ cup soy milk
2 tablespoons soy yogurt
1½ teaspoons finely grated lemon zest
¼ cup finely chopped crystallized ginger

DIRECTIONS

1. Preheat oven to 350°F. Line a muffin pan with paper cupcake liners.

2. Sift the flour, baking powder, baking soda, ginger, cinnamon, cloves, and salt into a bowl and mix.

3. Whisk the oil, molasses, maple syrup, soy milk, yogurt, and lemon zest in a separate large bowl. Add the flour mixture to the wet ingredients and mix just until smooth. Fold in the chopped crystallized ginger.

4. Fill cupcake liners two-thirds full. Bake for 19 to 22 minutes, until a knife or toothpick inserted into the center comes out clean. Transfer to a cooling rack and let cool completely before frosting.

**Gingerbread Cupcakes with
Lemony Buttercream Frosting**

CRIMSON VELVETEEN CUPCAKES
with *Old-Fashioned Velvet Icing*

WE'VE SEEN A lot of radioactively-hued baked goods out there calling themselves Red Velvet, but personally we prefer the hint of cocoa and generous helping of vanilla in these tender, fluffy cupcakes with the intriguing burgundy color. Top them with either OLD-FASHIONED VELVET FROSTING (recipe follows), VEGAN FLUFFY BUTTERCREAM FROSTING (page 142), or VEGAN CREAM CHEESE FROSTING (page 158).

INGREDIENTS

1 cup soy milk
1 teaspoon apple cider vinegar
1¼ cups all-purpose flour
1 cup granulated sugar
2 tablespoons cocoa powder, dutched-processed or regular
½ teaspoon baking powder
½ teaspoon baking soda
½ teaspoon salt
⅓ cup canola oil
2 tablespoons red food coloring
2 teaspoons vanilla extract
¼ teaspoon almond extract
1 teaspoon chocolate extract (see Sprinkle Tip below)

OLD-FASHIONED VELVET ICING
(recipe follows)
⅓ cup finely chopped pecans, for garnish

DIRECTIONS

1. Preheat oven 350°F and line muffin pans with cupcake liners.
2. Whisk together the soy milk and vinegar and set aside to curdle.
3. Sift the flour, sugar, cocoa, baking powder, baking soda, and salt into a large bowl and mix.
4. Add the oil, food coloring, chocolate extract, and almond extract to the curdled soy milk. Whisk well to combine. Gently fold wet ingredients into dry, mixing until large lumps disappear.
5. Fill cupcake liners about two-thirds of the way full as these cupcakes will rise fairly high. Place in hot oven and bake 18 to 20 minutes

OLD-FASHIONED VELVET ICING

MAKE 12 CUPCAKES

LIKE THE NAME says, this is a vegan spin on a traditional cooked icing. It's not as fluffy as a buttercream, yet has a smooth, creamy, custardlike consistency. Be absolutely sure to completely cool the cooked flour mixture before beating in the shortening and margarine, or you'll have frosting soup. As when making a buttercream frosting, an electric mixer is essential for getting the right consistency.

2 tablespoons all-purpose flour
½ cup soy milk
¼ cup nonhydrogenated shortening
¼ cup margarine
2 teaspoons vanilla extract
1 cup superfine or castor sugar

1. In a small saucepan over medium heat, whisk together the flour and soy milk. Stir constantly until the mixture starts to thicken and has a puddinglike consistency, about 3 to 4 minutes. Remove from heat and allow to cool 2 minutes. Transfer to a large bowl and press plastic wrap onto the top of custard to prevent a skin from forming. Allow mixture to cool completely before next step. (This is very important, as warm pudding might melt the fats).

2. Cream together the shortening, margarine, vanilla, and sugar then beat in cold custard. Beat with electric mixer for 4 to 6 minutes; frosting should become lighter in color and have a very creamy texture, similar to very thick whipped cream. Frost on cooled cupcakes and sprinkle tops with chopped pecans.

until done, but be sure not to over-bake. Let cool for a few minutes and transfer to a cooling rack to cool completely.

TO ASSEMBLE:

1. Frost Crimson Velveteen Cupcakes with OLD-FASHIONED VELVET ICING and sprinkle tops with chopped pecans. Keep frosted cupcakes refrigerated until 10 to 15 minutes before serving.

Sprinkles

Chocolate extract isn't always easy to find but it's really worth the trouble in this recipe. Avoid artificial chocolate extract at all costs, however. If real chocolate extract is nowhere to be found, just incread the amount of vanilla extract to 2½ teaspoons and almond extract to ½ teaspoon.

Peanut Butter Cupcakes

PEANUT BUTTER CUPCAKES

MAKES 12 CUPCAKES

WE ALSO CALL these Jimmy Carter Cakes, because he was a peanut farmer and he loves solar energy. But no one cares about that. What they do care about is that these cupcakes are pushed to maximum peanuty capacity and still remain moist and fluffy. And that is almost as important as solar energy.

INGREDIENTS

¾ cup soy milk

2 teaspoons apple cider vinegar

½ cup natural chunky peanut butter

⅓ cup canola oil

⅔ cup granulated sugar

2 tablespoons dark molasses

1 teaspoon vanilla extract

2 teaspoons ground flaxseed

1 cup plus 2 tablespoons all-purpose flour

1 teaspoon baking powder

½ teaspoon baking soda

¼ teaspoon salt

QUICK MELTY GANACHE (page 160)

¼ cup chopped peanuts, for garnish

DIRECTIONS

1. Preheat oven to 350°F. Line a muffin pan with cupcake liners.

2. Mix soy milk with vinegar in a measuring cup and set aside to curdle.

3. In a large mixing bowl, cream the peanut butter, oil, sugar, molasses, vanilla, and ground flaxseeds until well combined. Add the soy milk mixture and mix until incorporated.

4. Sift the flour, baking powder, baking soda, and salt into a separate bowl and mix. Add the dry ingredients to the wet and mix until just combined.

5. Fill cupcake liners two-thirds full. Bake for 23 to 26 minutes. Remove from oven and transfer to cooling racks.

TO ASSEMBLE:

1. Place Quick Melty Ganache in a pastry bag fitted with a small hole. Pipe the ganache on in a zigzag or swirly pattern (see page 25). Alternatively, you can just spoon it on and call it a day. Sprinkle with chopped nuts. Place cupcakes in the fridge to set for about 10 minutes.

CHOCOLATE CHERRY CRÈME CUPCAKES

MAKES 12 CUPCAKES

LOADED WITH JUICY dark cherries and VEGAN FLUFFY BUTTERCREAM FROSTING (page 142), this variation on YOUR BASIC CHOCOLATE CUPCAKES goes beyond cute little cupcake into the territory of serious dessert. Try the Black Forest variation with the outrageous addition of cherry brandy. These are easy and super fun to make, using the super top secret patented Isa and Terry Cupcake Excavation Method® as seen in the TIRAMISÙ CUPCAKES (page 119).

INGREDIENTS

YOUR BASIC CHOCOLATE CUPCAKES
  (page 37)

For Saucy Cherries:
- 1 (10-ounce) bag frozen cherries, thawed
- 2 tablespoons granulated sugar
- 1 tablespoon arrowroot
- 3 tablespoons pomegranate juice or water

VEGAN FLUFFY BUTTERCREAM FROSTING
  (page 142), about 1½ cups of prepared frosting
Chopped or shaved chocolate, for garnish
6 candied cherries, cut in half, for decorating, optional

DIRECTIONS

TO MAKE SAUCY CHERRIES:

1. In a saucepan over medium heat, combine thawed cherries and their juice, and sugar. Stir till mixture starts to simmer, about 4 to 5 minutes. Whisk together arrowroot and pomegranate juice in a small bowl or cup, then steadily pour into the cherries, stirring constantly. Keep stirring; the mixture will rapidly thicken. Remove from heat and allow to fully cool to room temperature.

TO ASSEMBLE:

1. With a tablespoon (the large kind you eat soup with or the kind you measure with) or a paring knife, carefully dig a neat cone out of the top of each cooled cupcake. Set aside the cones. Load refrigerated Vegan Fluffy Buttercream Frosting into a pastry bag fitted with a large star tip.

2. Spoon about 2 to 3 cherries plus sauce in the well of each cupcake. Distribute any remaining sauce and cherries among the cakes. Add a small dollop (roughly a tablespoon) of frosting on top of cherries, then gently but firmly place the tops onto the cupcakes. Pipe another dollop of frosting onto tops, sprinkle with chocolate and add a cherry on top if desired. These cupcakes taste best if allowed to sit for an hour before serving.

Variation:

BLACK FOREST CUPCAKES: Add 1 tablespoon kirsch cherry brandy to Your Basic Chocolate Cupcakes batter, when you add the vanilla. Add an additional tablespoon of kirsch to the saucy cherries after you've removed them from the heat. Lastly, brush Kirsch Glaze (recipe follows) onto cupcakes, dribbling a small amount in the cupcake "well" before filling with cherries and brushing any remaining glaze on top of cakes before frosting.

★ ★ ★

KIRSCH GLAZE

3 tablespoons kirsch
1 tablespoon granulated sugar

DIRECTIONS

1. Combine 2 tablespoons water, kirsch, and sugar in a small saucepan. Bring the mixture to boil over medium heat, stirring occasionally. Reduce heat and simmer for 2 minutes, then remove from heat to cool. Use while warm on cupcakes.

Left to right: **Blueberry Lemon Crème Cupcakes, Chocolate Cherry Crème Cupcakes, Strawberry Tallcakes**

Brooklyn vs. Boston Cream Pie Cakes

BROOKLYN vs. BOSTON CREAM PIE CAKES

MAKES 12 CUPCAKES

WE'RE NOT TRYING to start any trouble between Boston and Brooklyn here. Instead one might say we've reinvented the classic combination golden cake, vanilla custard, and rich chocolate icing and made it better with a little veganization and in the perfect form of a cupcake.

The Vanilla Vegan Pastry Crème is not as thick as a frosting, so filling these cupcakes might get a little messy. This recipe makes a generous amount of creme, so don't be stingy when filling those cupcakes. These cupcakes taste best if allowed to chill for at least an hour before serving. The chocolate ganache topping might look a little dull straight out of the cold, so allow cupcakes to sit at room temperature for about 15 minutes to give their surfaces that pretty shine again.

INGREDIENTS

GOLDEN VANILLA CUPCAKES (page 33)
RICH CHOCOLATE GANACHE TOPPING
(page 143)

For the Vanilla Vegan Pastry Crème:
½ cup soy milk
½ teaspoon agar powder, or 1½ teaspoons agar flakes
4 teaspoons arrowroot
6 ounces soft silken tofu (about half
of a Mori-Nu package), gently
pressed to remove excess water
⅓ cup superfine or castor sugar
Pinch salt
1½ teaspoons vanilla extract

DIRECTIONS

**TO MAKE THE VANILLA VEGAN
PASTRY CRÈME:**

1. Pour ⅓ cup soy milk into a small saucepan; keep the remaining soy milk in the measuring cup. Sprinkle agar powder over the soy milk in the saucepan and cook mixture over medium heat, stirring constantly. Bring mixture to a boil, reduce heat, and continue to cook for about 4 minutes. The agar will be dissolved when the soy milk appears smooth,

and a spoon dipped into the mixture does not have any undissolved agar flakes or powder flecks sticking to the spoon.

2. Whisk the powdered arrowroot into the remaining soy milk in the measuring cup. Pour the arrowroot mixture into the agar mixture in a steady stream, stirring the whole time. The mixture will cook and get very thick in 1 to 2 minutes, and when done it will resemble a very thick pudding. Remove from heat and set aside. Place it in the refrigerator and allow it to set for at least an hour.

3. Crumble tofu into a blender, add the sugar, salt, and cooked arrowroot mixture. Blend till creamy. Add vanilla extract and blend again. Scrape mixture into a container, cover, and put in refrigerator to chill and firm up, at least an hour.

TO ASSEMBLE:

1. Make a hole in the center of each Golden Vanilla Cupcake by poking with your finger. Very gently press the sides and bottom of the hole to make it a little larger. You'll want the space to be able to fill in with lots of custard.

2. Fit a pastry bag with a large round or star-tipped nozzle, then fill bag with firmed Vegan Vanilla Pastry Crème. Fill only halfway to make handling the bag easier.

3. Fill each cupcake with pastry crème, trying to get as much filling as possible into the cupcakes. Cupcakes should feel noticeably heavier. Remove any excess crème on top by wiping with a knife or finger. Spread tops of cupcakes with RICH CHOCOLATE GANACHE TOPPING. For smoother looking tops, try applying two thin layers of ganache instead of one thick layer to tops of cupcakes. Chill for an hour before serving.

Sprinkles

Powdered agar is much better for this recipe than flaked. It dissolves and cooks much faster. If all you can find is flaked, the cooking time will be longer, as much as 10 minutes. Just soak the agar in the soy milk for 15 minutes before heating, stir often, and watch very carefully so as to not burn the soy milk.

MAPLE CUPCAKES

with *Creamy Maple Frosting* and *Sugared Walnuts*

MAKE 12 CUPCAKES

WHERE WOULD WE be without maple syrup? There would be no happiness or joy, we would be eating a lot of dry pancakes and waffles, and most certainly we wouldn't be eating these scrumptious cupcakes that strike a perfect balance between sweet, mapley, and nutty. The addition of candied walnuts is extra special, but if you can't be bothered at least toast them lightly before chopping.

INGREDIENTS

½ cup soy milk
½ teaspoon apple cider vinegar
1⅓ cups all-purpose flour
¾ teaspoon baking powder
½ teaspoon baking soda
½ teaspoon salt
¼ teaspoon ground nutmeg
½ cup maple syrup
⅓ cup canola oil
2 tablespoons brown sugar
1¼ teaspoon maple extract
½ teaspoon vanilla extract
½ cup SUGARED WALNUTS (recipe follows), finely chopped (measure first, then chop)
CREAMY MAPLE FROSTING (recipe follows)

For the Sugared Walnuts:

1 cup walnut halves
⅓ cup granulated sugar
3 tablespoons maple syrup
Dash salt
Dash ground cinnamon

DIRECTIONS

TO MAKE THE SUGARED WALNUTS:

1. Preheat the oven to 275°F. Spread the walnuts on a rimmed baking sheet and toast in the oven for 6 to 8 minutes. Open oven and shake the pan after about 4 minutes. Watch carefully so as not to burn! Remove from oven and place in a bowl to cool. Lightly grease a large piece of parchment paper and have

it ready because you will need it at the end of the next step.

2. Pour sugar, maple syrup, and salt into a large, cold, heavy-bottom skillet. Turn heat to medium and stir with a wooden spoon till sugar starts to melt and bubble, about 5 minutes. Continue stirring and cook another 3 to 4 minutes until mixture is thick, amber-brown, and smells like caramel. Remove from heat and quickly stir in the walnuts and cinnamon, stirring to coat each nut. Immediately spread coated walnuts on greased parchment paper, using a spatula to spread out the nuts and avoid forming large clusters. Allow to cool completely on sheet before handling or eating.

TO MAKE CUPCAKES:

1. Preheat oven to 350°F. Line a muffin pan with cupcake liners.

2. Whisk together the soy milk and vinegar in a large bowl; set aside and allow to curdle for a few minutes.

✳ *Sprinkles* ✳

✦ While we normally hate flavored soy milk powder, if you have vanilla soy milk powder this is the place to use it—it gives the frosting a luscious hue and great flavor. Just sift out the larger sugar crystals before using. Discard sifted crystals, or use for baking.

✦ Whole wheat pastry works especially well in this recipe. Replace up to half of the flour with whole wheat pastry flour.

3. Sift the flour, baking powder, baking soda, salt, and nutmeg into a separate bowl and mix. Whisk the maple syrup, oil, brown sugar, and vanilla, and maple extract into the soy milk mixture. Form a well in the dry ingredients and pour in wet ingredients, stirring till large lumps are gone; fold in chopped sugared walnuts. Fill cupcake liners two-thirds of the way. Bake 20 to 22 minutes. Transfer to cooling racks to cool completely. Frost with CREAMY MAPLE FROSTING and sprinkle with Sugared Walnuts.

CREAMY MAPLE FROSTING

⅔ cup maple syrup
¾ cup margarine, softened
⅔ cup soy milk powder
1 teaspoon maple extract
1 teaspoon vanilla extract

DIRECTIONS

1. Beat together the softened margarine and maple syrup. It might look a little curdly but that's okay. Beat in the vanilla and the maple extract, then slowly add soy milk powder a little bit at a time. The frosting should be creamy and fluffy. If it looks too wet, add a little more soy milk powder, if too stiff, drizzle in a little more maple syrup. The frosting can be stored in fridge till ready to use, just allow to sit at room temperature 10 minutes to soften.

PINEAPPLE RIGHT-SIDE-UP CUPCAKES

MAKES 12 CUPCAKES

THESE ARE SUBLIME summertime cupcakes, perfect straight out of the fridge and eaten while lounging about poolside, or sitting on your fire escape with your feet dunked in a bowl of cold water. Pineapple makes an appearance in the delicately spiced cake and as the refreshing and luscious topping.

INGREDIENTS

For the cupcakes:
- 1 cup all-purpose flour
- 1 teaspoon baking powder
- ¼ teaspoon salt
- ½ teaspoon ground cinnamon
- ½ teaspoon ground ginger
- ¼ teaspoon ground allspice
- 1 cup crushed pineapple (in its own juice)
- ¼ cup canola oil
- ½ cup plus 2 tablespoons granulated sugar
- 1 teaspoon vanilla extract
- 12 maraschino cherries or fresh raspberries, for garnish

For the topping:
- 1 cup crushed pineapple (in its own juice)
- ¼ cup sugar
- 1 tablespoon tapioca flour, cornstarch, or arrowroot
- ½ teaspoon vanilla extract

DIRECTIONS

TO MAKE THE CUPCAKES:

1. Preheat oven to 350°F. Line a muffin pan with cupcake liners.
2. Sift the flour, baking powder, salt, cinnamon, ginger, and allspice into a large bowl.
3. Combine the pineapple, oil, sugar, and vanilla in a blender and puree. Make a well in the center of the flour mixture and add the wet ingredients. Mix well; there may be some pineapple clumps that weren't pureed and that's fine.

4. Pour batter into cupcake liners so that they are just over half full. You need to leave some space after they rise because the pineapple topping is gooey (in a good way). Bake for 25 to 27 minutes.

5. Let cupcakes cool for about 10 minutes then move them to a cutting board or a tray that will fit on a shelf in your fridge.

TO MAKE THE TOPPING:

1. Combine all ingredients in a small saucepan. Bring to a boil, and stir constantly for about 30 seconds. Bring the heat down to low and stir for one more minute. Immediately use a tablespoon to scoop the topping onto the cupcakes. The topping will spread but you can help it along with the back of the spoon. Place a raspberry or maraschino cherry in the center of each cupcake.

2. Place in the fridge for about 30 minutes or until ready to serve.

Chocolate Mint Cupcakes

CHOCOLATE MINT CUPCAKES

MAKES 12 CUPCAKES

THESE ARE LIKE those chocolate-covered mint patties that the kids love so much. You absolutely can't eat mint icing on its own, it needs the chocolate ganache to bring it all together. But once it is brought, it is heavenly.

INGREDIENTS

YOUR BASIC CHOCOLATE CUPCAKE (page 37), with 1 teaspoon mint extract added to the wet ingredients

For the Mint Icing:
¼ cup nonhydrogenated shortening
3 cups confectioners' sugar (sifted if clumpy)
¼ cup plus 1 tablespoon soy creamer or soy milk
1½ teaspoons mint extract
½ teaspoon vanilla extract
Small drop green food coloring liquid or paste
QUICK MELTY GANACHE (page 160)

DIRECTIONS

TO MAKE THE MINT ICING:

1. Cream the shortening for a few seconds to soften it. We found that it's easier to do this with a fork than with a handheld mixer.

2. Add 1 cup powdered sugar and a splash (tablespoon or so) of soy creamer and mix to incorporate. Alternately add sugar and creamer, mixing after each addition, until all the ingredients are used and the icing is smooth and creamy. Add the mint and vanilla extracts and coloring; mix to incorporate.

TO ASSEMBLE:

1. When cupcakes have fully cooled, fill a pastry bag fitted with a #21 star tip with Mint Icing. Pipe the icing onto the cupcake in a spiral from outside in, leaving a little room on the sides for the cupcake to show

through. Let the icing set while you prepare the QUICK MELTY GANACHE.

2. Let the ganache cool to room temperature, stirring every once in a while to keep it smooth. Don't use it while it is still hot or it will melt your mint icing. Use a tablespoon to dollop (or plop, whichever you prefer) ganache on top of cupcakes. The chocolate should fall in the center and drip down a bit so that the pretty mint icing spiral shows through. Decorate immediately with:

- a mint Newman-O
- a chocolate candy lentil
- a rose of mint icing
- a spearmint gumdrop
- a sprig of fresh mint

3. Refrigerate for 15 to 30 minutes to let the ganache set before serving.

S'MORES CUPCAKES

WE MAY BE city girls but we love us some campfires. And not just because we like to steal people's bras and hide them in trees. These cupcakes will bring out the rustic survivalist in you—the rustic survivalist that knows from scrumptious cupcakes.

INGREDIENTS

¾ cup brown sugar
½ cup canola oil
2 tablespoons molasses
¼ cup soy yogurt
1¼ cups soy milk
1 teaspoon vanilla extract
1 cup all-purpose flour
1 teaspoon baking powder
½ teaspoon baking soda
½ teaspoon ground cinnamon
¼ teaspoon salt
½ cup graham cracker crumbs (see Sprinkles, below)

For the topping:
QUICK MELTY GANACHE (page 160) or
SHAVED CHOCOLATE (page 29)
VEGAN FLUFFY BUTTERCREAM FROSTING
(page 142)

6 graham cracker rectangles, broken in half
Extra graham cracker crumbs

DIRECTIONS

1. Preheat oven to 350°F. Line a muffin pan with cupcake liners.
2. Mix the brown sugar, oil, molasses, yogurt, soy milk, and vanilla in a large bowl.
3. Sift the flour, baking powder, baking soda, cinnamon, and salt into a separate bowl and mix. Add the graham cracker crumbs and mix it up.
4. Add the dry ingredients to the wet in three batches, mixing well after each addition.

5. Fill cupcake liners full. Bake for 22 to 25 minutes, or until a toothpick inserted in the center of one comes out clean. Transfer to a cooling rack and let cool completely before decorating.

TO ASSEMBLE:

1. Spread or pipe a thick layer of VEGAN FLUFFY BUTTERCREAM FROSTING onto each cupcake. We like to use a wide decorating tip to create a swirly mountain of yumminess. Sprinkle graham cracker crumbs over the frosting. Drizzle with ganache or sprinkle with shaved chocolate and stick a graham cracker into each cupcake. You can eat immediately for the authentic s'mores warm chocolate thing or allow to set. It tastes yummy either way.

✳ *Sprinkles* ✳

✦ To rapidly make graham cracker crumbs, crumble six whole graham crackers into a food processor and process into crumbs. Measure out the ½ cup and save the rest of the crumbs for decorative purposes. If you don't have a food processor and can't find prepackaged vegan graham cracker crumbs, then place graham crackers in a plastic bag and cover with a dish towel. Use a kitchen mallet or a plain old hammer to smash the crackers into fine crumbs. You may need to shake the bag a few times to make sure you get them all.

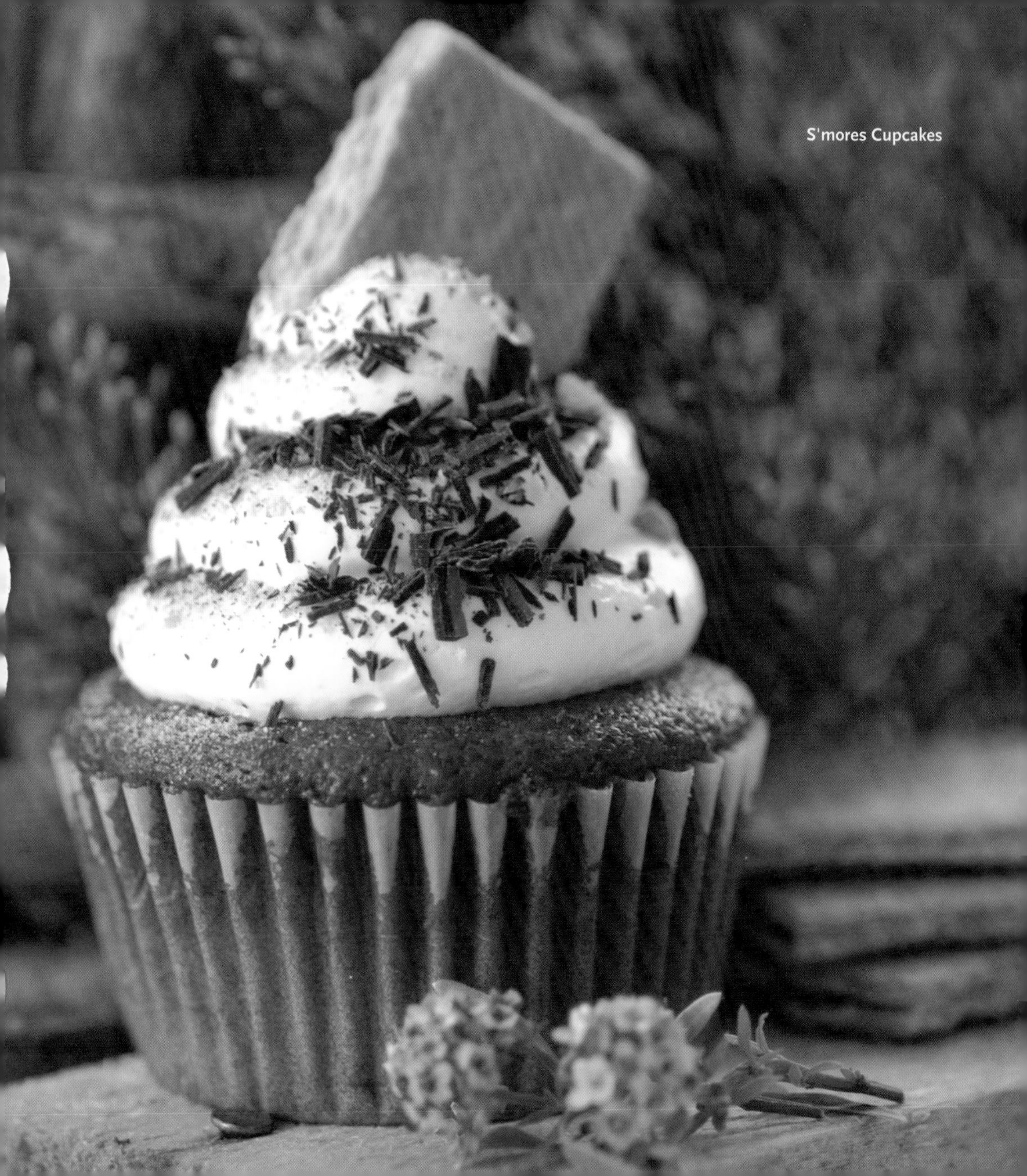

S'mores Cupcakes

BROOKLYN BROWNIE CUPCAKES

MAKES 15 CUPCAKES

THIS IS OUR top secret brownie recipe converted to cupcakes. They are puffier than we normally make cupcakes but we like them that way—the tops get all crackled and brownielike. Serve them pure and unfrosted, lightly sprinkled with powdered sugar, or spread with a thin layer of chocolate frosting and chopped walnuts. The cherry and bourbon are not pronounced flavors; they just add a greater depth to the chocolate. This recipe makes fifteen cupcakes so have handy some foil cupcake liners to cook a few solo. Don't overfill the liners or your perfect brownies will sink!

INGREDIENTS

⅔ cup semisweet chocolate chips
¼ cup soy yogurt
½ cup black cherry preserves
½ cup soy milk
¾ cup granulated sugar
½ cup canola oil
1 teaspoon vanilla extract
½ teaspoon almond extract
2 tablespoons bourbon, or any whiskey
1 cup plus 2 tablespoons all-purpose flour
¼ cup Dutch-processed cocoa powder
1 teaspoon baking powder
½ teaspoon baking soda
¼ teaspoon salt
Chopped walnuts, for garnish

For the Chocolate Brownie Frosting:
2 tablespoons melted margarine
¼ cup Dutch-processed cocoa powder
3 tablespoons soy milk
1 teaspoon vanilla extract
1½ cups confectioners' sugar

DIRECTIONS

1. Preheat oven to 350°F. Line a muffin pan with cupcake liners and spray each liner with nonstick cooking spray.

2. Melt the chocolate either in a double boiler (if you're lucky enough to have one), the microwave (again,

lucky), or a small pan over very low heat.

3. Mix the yogurt, preserves, soy milk, sugar, oil, vanilla, almond extract, and bourbon in a large bowl. The preserves should be mixed in very well and there should be no large clumps.

4. Sift in the flour, cocoa, baking powder, baking soda, and salt. Mix thoroughly—if using a handheld mixer, mix for about 3 minutes on medium speed. Incorporate the melted chocolate.

5. Fill the liners full with batter. Bake for 24 to 26 minutes. The tops may come out looking shiny, soft, and undone but that is okay; they should look that way. Transfer to a cooling rack and let cool completely before frosting.

TO MAKE THE CHOCOLATE BROWNIE FROSTING:

1. Beat together the margarine, cocoa, soy milk, and vanilla. Add the sugar in cupfuls until incorporated. You can use immediately or refrigerate until ready to use it. If refrigerated, bring frosting back to room temperature or it won't spread correctly.

TO ASSEMBLE:

1. Spread a layer of frosting onto each cupcake and sprinkle with chopped walnuts. Keep brownies in a cool place until ready to serve.

Banana Split Cupcakes and
"The Elvis" variation

BANANA SPLIT CUPCAKES

MAKES 12 CUPCAKES

LOADS OF FLUFFY white icing, a ribbon of fruity preserves, and chocolate, nuts, ganache, and sprinkles give these an unmistakably scrumptious cupcake profile. One tester described the contrasting flavors and textures in this cupcake as a "party in your mouth," and we can attest that cleaning up after this party beats picking up beer bottles off the living room floor any day. Pureeing the mashed banana gives these cupcakes a delicate crumb and light texture that sets them apart from other banana baked goods.

This is also a great basic banana cupcake. It's just begging to be to topped or stuffed with VEGAN FLUFFY BUTTERCREAM FROSTING and cocoa, COCONUT PECAN FUDGE FROSTING (page 147), a thin glaze of RICH CHOCOLATE GANACHE TOPPING (page 143), or see below for the always popular "Elvis" cupcake.

INGREDIENTS
- ½ cup pineapple preserves
- ½ cup very ripe banana, mashed well (the darker and browner the banana the better!)
- 1¼ cups all-purpose flour
- ¼ teaspoon baking soda
- 1 teaspoon baking powder
- ½ teaspoon salt
- ¾ cup granulated sugar
- ⅓ cup canola oil
- ⅔ cup rice milk
- 1½ teaspoons vanilla extract
- ½ teaspoon almond extract
- ¼ cup finely chopped dark chocolate

VEGAN FLUFFY BUTTERCREAM FROSTING (page 142)

QUICK MELTY GANACHE (page 160)
- ¼ cup finely chopped walnuts
- Chocolate or rainbow sprinkles
- 6 candied cherries, cut in half, optional

DIRECTIONS
1. Preheat oven to 350°F. Line muffin pan with paper liners.
2. Stir pineapple preserves in a small saucepan over low heat till melted and they pour easily when scooped

up with a spoon. Remove from heat and set aside.

3. Push the mashed bananas through a sieve or blend for a few seconds with an immersion or regular blender to get rid of any remaining lumps. It should be fairly smooth.

4. Sift the flour, baking soda, baking powder, salt, and sugar in a large bowl and mix. In a separate, smaller bowl, whisk together the oil, rice milk, vanilla, almond extract, and mashed banana. Create a well in the dry ingredients and fold in wet ingredients, mixing to just combine—don't over-mix (very small lumps are okay).

5. Fill liners two-thirds full. Top the batter of each cupcake with 1 teaspoon melted preserves and 1 teaspoon chopped chocolate. With a small knife, carefully stir each cupcake two or three times to swirl in preserves and chocolate. Bake for 20 to 22 minutes till knife inserted into cupcake comes out clean. Cool completely on wire rack before frosting.

TO ASSEMBLE:

1. Top cooled cupcakes with VEGAN FLUFFY BUTTERCREAM FROSTING; this looks best when piled high with a pastry bag fitted with a large star nozzle. Drizzle QUICK MELTY GANACHE over frosting, sprinkle with nuts and sprinkles, then top with a cherry, if desired.

Variations:

"THE ELVIS": Make plain banana cupcake following the recipe above, omitting preserves and chocolate from batter. Prepare a double batch of PEANUT BUTTERCREAM (page 151). Fill cupcakes with frosting (using the method described for BROOKLYN VS. BOSTON CREAM PIE CAKES on page 65) and top with remaining frosting. Top with chopped roasted peanuts (plain or salted), and decorate with either fresh banana slices or banana chips.

TROPICAL PARADISE: Either frost plain banana cupcakes with COCONUT GLAZE (page 122) or top with PINEAPPLE TOPPING (page 70) and thin slices of fresh kiwi.

CHOCOLATE AND VANILLA MARBLE CUPCAKES

THESE CUPCAKES ARE not unlike the marble cakes that adorn the windows of the Jewish bakeries around our parts. We top these with single dollops of VEGAN FLUFFY BUTTERCREAM FROSTING (page 142) so that you can see the pretty, swirly marble patterns underneath, so you only need half a batch of the frosting. Pipe 'em out with the biggest star tube you've got and be prepared to get a little messy when making these.

INGREDIENTS

1 teaspoon apple cider vinegar

1 cup soy milk

½ cup margarine, softened

¾ cup plus 2 tablespoons granulated sugar

1 teaspoon vanilla extract

½ teaspoon almond extract

1 tablespoon cornstarch

1½ cups all-purpose flour

1½ teaspoons baking powder

¼ teaspoon salt

2 tablespoons plus 1 teaspoon cocoa powder (Dutch-processed is best because it is darkest)

DIRECTIONS

1. Preheat oven to 350°F. Line a muffin pan with cupcake liners.

2. Add the vinegar to soy milk in a liquid measuring cup and set aside to curdle.

3. Sift flour, baking powder, and salt into a separate bowl.

4. In a separate medium bowl, cream the margarine for a minute or so. Add the sugar and cream for 3 to 5 minutes, until light and fluffy. Add the vanilla. almond extract, and cornstarch and mix to combine. Alternately add some of the milk mixture, then some of the flour mixture, and mix with a hand

blender for about 15 seconds, incorporating the ingredients well after each addition. It should take about three batches of each to combine everything. Mix until the batter is smooth.

5. Fill a saucepan with 1 inch of water and bring to a boil. Put the cocoa powder in yet another mixing bowl. Add 3 tablespoons of the boiled water to the cocoa powder and whisk until smooth. Take 1 cup of the batter and add it to the cocoa. Mix together until the batter is chocolatey.

6. This is where things get messy. For the best marbled pattern, take two separate small measuring cups and fill one with vanilla batter and one with chocolate batter. Add both to the cupcake liner at the same time, side by side. Some people may not have the hand-eye coordination to do this (as easy as it sounds) so if this is the case, just alternately drop in a spoonful of vanilla to one side and spoonful of chocolate to the other as best you can. Continue until there is no more batter left— you will end up with a spoonful of vanilla on top because there is more vanilla batter. The liners should be full.

7. Use a toothpick or a butter knife to swirl in marble patterns. My best tip for this is to go in a clockwise direction around the edge of the liner, then switch to a counter-clockwise direction and spiral toward the center.

8. Bake for 24 to 26 minutes, until a knife or a toothpick inserted through the center of one comes out clean.

9. Transfer to a cooling rack and let cool completely before frosting.

FANCY CUPCAKES

INGREDIENTS LIKE GREEN tea, fresh lime, stout, rosewater, and more make these cupcakes sometimes exotic, sometimes unusual, but always delightful. We don't mean to suggest the following recipes are too fancy for everyday use or any more difficult to prepare than traditional favorites. On the contrary, many of these recipes are simple to make, but result in wildly different and delicious cupcakes. Only a few recipes are a bit trickier or have a few more steps than most, but are worth your precious time and effort.

Toasted Coconut Cupcakes with
Coffee Buttercream Frosting

TOASTED COCONUT CUPCAKES

with *Coffee Buttercream Frosting*

MAKES 12 CUPCAKES

THESE ARE FOR our friend Jimbles; he loves the coconut, chocolate, coffee combination and wanted us to call them ChoCofCos. We declined the title but obliged with these little bites of heaven. This batter is a little thicker than most cake batters so don't panic and think you did something wrong.

INGREDIENTS

- 1 cup all-purpose flour
- ⅓ cup cocoa powder
- 1½ teaspoons baking powder
- ¼ teaspoon salt
- ¼ cup coconut oil
- 1 cup coconut milk
- ¾ cup granulated sugar
- 1 teaspoon vanilla extract
- 2 teaspoon coconut extract
- ½ cup unsweetened shredded coconut
- TOASTED COCONUT (recipe below)
- COFFEE BUTTERCREAM FROSTING (recipe below)
- Chocolate-covered coffee beans, optional

DIRECTIONS

1. Preheat oven to 350°F, line muffin pan with cupcake liners.

2. In a medium bowl, sift together flour, cocoa, baking powder, and salt.

3. Melt the coconut oil in a small saucepan over very low heat. Once melted, turn the heat off but leave it in the pan on the stove so that it stays warm and does not solidify.

4. In a separate medium bowl mix together coconut milk, sugar, vanilla, and coconut extract. Stir in the melted coconut oil. Add the flour mixture in batches, beating well after each addition. Mix until smooth, then fold in the shredded coconut.

5. Fill cupcake liners two-thirds full. Bake for 24 to 26 minutes. Transfer to a wire rack and cool completely.

TO ASSEMBLE:

1. Spread a generous amount of Coffee Buttercream Frosting on cooled cupcakes. Roll the frosted cupcake along its rim in the Toasted Coconut to create a ring around the circumference.

2. Add chocolate-covered coffee beans or coffee lentils to the center to decorate if you wish.

★ ★ ★

TOASTED COCONUT

½ cup unsweetened shredded coconut

DIRECTIONS

1. Preheat a small frying pan over medium heat for about 2 minutes.

2. Pour the coconut into the pan, to stir constantly with a spatula. The coconut will begin to turn honey brown. Keep stirring and tossing for about 1½ minutes to get all the coconut evenly toasted. Turn off the heat and keep stirring and tossing for 30 seconds more. Once uniformly toasted, transfer to a plate and spread out to cool.

★ ★ ★

COFFEE BUTTERCREAM FROSTING

¼ cup nonhydrogenated shortening
¼ cup nonhydrogenated margarine, softened
2 cups confectioners' sugar
2 tablespoons coconut milk or soy milk
1½ teaspoons coffee extract
½ teaspoon vanilla extract

DIRECTIONS

1. Beat the shortening and margarine together until combined well and fluffy. Alternately add the sugar and coconut milk to the shortening mixture, beating well after each addition. Add the coffee extract and vanilla and beat until light and fluffy, about 3 minutes with a handheld mixer on low-medium speed, or 5 to 7 minutes if you're using a fork. Refrigerate until ready to use.

APRICOT-GLAZED ALMOND CUPCAKES

MAKES 12 CUPCAKES

THESE MIGHT BE overshadowed by the more "foofy" cupcakes in the book, but don't pass them up, they are rich, fragrant, and sophisticated. The sweet apricot preserve filling is baked right into the cake, which is rich and moist with almond goodness. It's then glazed with apricot and decorated with sliced almonds. Classy.

INGREDIENTS

⅓ cup canola oil
¾ cup granulated sugar
¼ cup soy yogurt
⅔ cup almond milk, soy milk, or rice milk
1 teaspoon vanilla extract
2 teaspoons almond extract
1 cup plus 2 tablespoons all-purpose flour
1½ teaspoon baking powder
½ teaspoon salt
⅓ cup almond meal
⅓ cup apricot preserves

For the glaze:
½ cup apricot preserves
1 tablespoon water
⅓ cup sliced almonds

DIRECTIONS

1. Preheat oven to 350°F. Line a muffin pan with cupcake liners.

2. In a large bowl, combine oil, sugar, yogurt, almond milk, vanilla, and almond extract.

3. Sift in the flour, baking powder, and salt. Mix until the batter is smooth. Add the almond meal and mix to combine.

4. Fill each cupcake liner two-thirds full. Using a ½ teaspoon measuring spoon, add apricot preserves to the center of each cupcake. Tap lightly on the preserves to get them mostly level with the cupcake batter.

5. Bake for 24 to 26 minutes. You can't really do the toothpick test here because there is apricot filling and it won't come out clean, but gently press the top with your finger, if it springs back it's done.

6. Transfer to a cooling rack and cool.

TO MAKE THE GLAZE:

1. Place the apricot preserves and 1 tablespoon water in a small saucepan over medium-low heat. Bring to a boil, stirring often. Boil for a minute. Turn the heat off and stir the glaze for another 30 seconds or so.

TO ASSEMBLE:

1. Use a pastry brush to apply glaze to the tops of the cupcakes. Sprinkle a single layer of almonds over the tops. Let cool before serving.

VEGAN CUPCAKES TAKE OVER THE WORLD

CHOCOLATE STOUT CUPCAKES

MAKES 12 CUPCAKES

WE LOVE TO bake with beer; it makes us feel tough. We also love crumb cake and chocolate so we figured the combination of both would blow our minds, and obviously it did.

INGREDIENTS

For the crumb topping:
- ¼ cup all-purpose flour
- ¼ cup Dutch-processed cocoa powder
- ¼ cup granulated sugar
- 2 tablespoons canola oil

For the cupcakes:
- ¾ cup soy milk
- 1 teaspoon apple cider vinegar
- 1 cup plus 2 tablespoons all-purpose flour
- ⅓ cup Dutch-processed cocoa powder
- ½ teaspoon baking soda
- ½ teaspoon baking powder
- ¼ teaspoon salt
- ¼ cup stout
- ¾ cup granulated sugar
- ⅓ cup canola oil
- 1½ teaspoons vanilla extract
- Confectioners' sugar for dusting the finished cupcakes, optional

DIRECTIONS

1. Preheat oven to 350°F and muffin pan with paper liners.

TO MAKE THE CRUMB TOPPING:

1. In a small bowl, sift together the flour, cocoa, and sugar. Slowly drizzle the oil in while constantly tossing the flour mixture with a fork. Crumbs will start to form. After all the oil has been added, toss and stir the crumbs with your fingers for about 30 seconds to make as many crumbs as possible. The end result should leave you with mostly big crumbs (almost ¼ inch in diameter) and a little loose flour left over. (If the mixture is getting too clumpy and heavy

before you've added all the oil, it's okay to stop adding it.)

TO MAKE THE CUPCAKES:

1. Whisk together soy milk and vinegar in a large bowl. In a separate bowl, sift the flour, cocoa powder, baking soda, baking powder, salt and mix. Add stout, sugar, oil, and vanilla to the soy milk mixture and beat till foamy. Add dry ingredients to wet in two batches and beat for about 2 minutes.

2. Pour batter into liners, filling them three-quarters of the way. Gently sprinkle the tops with crumb topping, being careful that the crumbs don't sink into the batter but rest on top of it. Bake 20 to 22 minutes. Transfer to cooling racks. Once cooled you can dust the tops with confectioners' sugar.

Sprinkles

There are plenty of vegan stouts out there. If you are ever in doubt, consult this list: www.veganconnection.com/ veganbeer.htm

DULCE SIN LECHE CUPCAKES

MAKES 12 CUPCAKES

WE LOVE THESE light-textured coconut milk cupcakes with a ribbon of homemade vegan "milk" caramel, a hint of lemon, and a sprinkle of coconut. When eating these we imagine we're on a tropical island vacation where tanned cabana boys are serving us lusciously Latin and Caribbean-style vegan desserts. Then we wake up to find ourselves roasting to death in our steamy little NYC apartments every summer. While the island breeze might be just a dream, these sublime little cupcakes remain a delicious reality.

The brown rice syrup used in the topping is essential for these and can't be substituted. It has a consistency and deep caramel flavor similar to dairy-based dulce de leche.

INGREDIENTS

- 1¼ cups all-purpose flour
- 1 teaspoon baking powder
- ¼ teaspoon baking soda
- ½ teaspoon salt
- ½ cup granulated sugar
- ¼ cup brown sugar, packed
- ⅓ cup oil
- ½ cup soy milk
- ½ cup coconut milk
- 2 teaspoons vanilla extract
- ½ teaspoon finely grated lemon zest
- DULCE SIN LECHE TOPPING (recipe follows)
- ¼ cup unsweetened shredded coconut

DIRECTIONS

1. Preheat oven to 350°F. Prepare DULCE SIN LECHE first and set aside to cool.

2. In a large bowl, sift together the flour, baking powder, baking soda, and salt. Add sugar and brown sugar and mix. Whisk together the oil, soy milk, coconut milk, lemon zest, and vanilla. Make a well in the center of the dry ingredients and pour in wet ingredients. Mix until relatively smooth.

3. Fill cupcake liners two-thirds of the way full. Pour 1 teaspoon of DULCE SIN LECHE on top of each cupcake, then use a butter knife to stir tops of cupcakes a few times to swirl the sauce. Bake for 22 to 25 minutes. Cool cupcakes for a few minutes and transfer to wire rack until lukewarm.

TO ASSEMBLE:

1. Spoon 2 to 3 teaspoons of DULCE SIN LECHE on top of lukewarm cupcakes. Sprinkle tops with shredded coconut for garnish. Topping will be very sticky; allow to sit for an hour and the DULCE SIN LECHE will firm up a little. Allow to cool completely before eating.

★ ★ ★

DULCE SIN LECHE

DIRECTIONS

1. Prepare BROWN RICE CARAMEL GLAZE (page 146), but whisk in ¼ cup brown sugar after arrowroot thickens, but before adding the brown rice syrup.

   OPTIONAL: Whisk in 1 teaspoon caramel extract along with the vanilla extract.

LEMON MACADAMIA CUPCAKES
with *Lemon Buttercream*

MAKES 12 CUPCAKES

YUMMY. LEMON. MACADAMIAS. If you can find vegan white chocolate chips, add half a cupful to make this flavor combo even more intense. We use roasted, lightly salted macadamias because they seem to be the easiest to find, but any macadamias you have will work.

INGREDIENTS

- ⅓ cup canola oil
- ¾ cup granulated sugar
- ¼ cup soy yogurt
- ⅓ cup soy milk
- ¼ cup lemon juice
- 1 tablespoon finely grated lemon zest
- 1 teaspoon vanilla extract
- 1 cup plus 2 tablespoons all-purpose flour
- ½ teaspoon baking powder
- ½ teaspoon baking soda
- ¼ teaspoon salt
- ⅓ cup roasted macadamia nuts, ground
- ½ cup roasted macadamia nuts, coarsely chopped
- LEMON BUTTERCREAM (recipe follows)

DIRECTIONS

1. Preheat oven to 350°F. Line a muffin pan with cupcake liners.
2. In a medium bowl, stir together oil, sugar, yogurt, and soy milk. Add the lemon juice, lemon zest, and vanilla. Mix to combine.
3. In a separate bowl, sift together flour, baking powder, baking soda, and salt. Add the flour to the liquid mixture in two batches, mixing well after each addition. Add the ground macadamia nuts and beat until well incorporated. Fold in the chopped macadamias.

4. Fill cupcake liners three-quarters of the way full. Bake for 20 to 22 minutes, until a toothpick or knife inserted through the center comes out clean.

5. Transfer to a cooling rack and let cool completely before frosting.

Sprinkles

To make ground macadamias, pulse the little guys a handful of times in a food processor until they resemble coarse crumbs.

★ ★ ★

LEMON BUTTERCREAM

¼ cup shortening
¼ cup margarine, softened
2 cups confectioners' sugar
2 tablespoons fresh lemon juice
2 teaspoons finely grated lemon zest
1 teaspoon vanilla extract

DIRECTIONS

1. In a small bowl, cream the shortening and margarine until well combined. Add the confectioners' sugar in roughly ½-cup additions. After each addition of sugar add a splash of lemon juice and beat well with a handheld mixer. Add vanilla and beat for another 3 to 5 minutes until smooth, creamy, and fluffy. Wrap tightly with plastic wrap and refrigerate until ready to use.

GREEN TEA CUPCAKES
with *Green Tea Glaze and Almond Flowers*

MAKES 12 CUPCAKES

THESE GORGEOUS LITTLE cupcakes are made with matcha green tea powder, a Japanese green tea that's been steamed and ground to a very fine and silky powder. Nothing else will do. It's a little pricey, but a little goes a long way in baking and making sweets. Well-stocked Korean, Japanese, or Pan-Asian markets should have it, but make sure to only use varieties that do not have any added sugar. Only pure powdered tea will produce the right flavor and color.

We like to decorate these GREEN TEA CUPCAKES with pink marzipan flowers, bringing to mind the Cherry Blossom Festival at the Brooklyn Botanic Garden. These cuties are easy and fun to make, and can be made a day or two before the cupcakes.

INGREDIENTS

- ½ cup soy yogurt
- ⅔ cup rice milk
- ¼ teaspoon vanilla extract
- ⅓ cup canola oil
- ½ teaspoon almond extract
- 1¼ cups all-purpose flour
- 1 teaspoon baking powder
- ¼ teaspoon baking soda
- 3 to 4 teaspoons matcha tea powder
- ¼ teaspoon salt
- ¾ cup granulated sugar
- GREEN TEA GLAZE (recipe below)
- ALMOND FLOWERS (recipe below)

DIRECTIONS

1. Preheat oven to 350°F and line cupcake pan with liners.
2. In a large bowl, whisk together the yogurt, rice milk, vanilla, oil, and almond extract, beating well to blend in yogurt. Sift in the flour, baking powder, baking soda, matcha powder, salt, and sugar. If using rice flour it will be a little lumpy. Beat a little longer to break up any large lumps. Fill liners two-thirds full and bake 20 minutes or until a toothpick inserted through the center of one

comes out clean. Cool on racks before topping with glaze.

TO ASSEMBLE:

1. Use a tablespoon to pour GREEN TEA GLAZE into the center of each cupcake. Spread out a bit with the back of the spoon but it's nice if you can see the green edges of the cupcake. Gently press petals together to form flowers; then gently set flowers into wet glaze on cupcakes. Garnish centers with a silver ball (dip one side of ball into wet glaze first to secure on flower). Let glaze set before serving.

※ *Sprinkles* ※

◆ This recipe also works well with a little ground rice flour (not sweet/glutinous rice flour). Replace up to ¼ cup of flour with rice flour. The mixture might look a little lumpier; just beat a little extra. Some small lumps are okay.

◆ We know we already said this, but make sure your tea is pure tea, not something mixed with sugar. The presweetened stuff just sort of disappears when baked and will not give the cupcakes that special green tea taste or color.

Green Tea Cupcakes
with Green Tea Glaze
and Almond Flowers

★ ★ ★

GREEN TEA GLAZE

2 tablespoons margarine
1 cup confectioners' sugar
⅛ to ¼ teaspoon matcha tea
    powder
1 to 2 tablespoons rice milk
¼ teaspoon almond extract
Drop of vanilla extract

DIRECTIONS

1. With a fork, beat margarine to fluff, then mix in confectioners' sugar and matcha to form a crumbly mixture. Slowly beat in 1 tablespoon rice milk, almond extract, and vanilla. If icing is too thick to spread, pour in additional rice milk a teaspoon at a time and mix till desired consistency is reached.

★ ★ ★

ALMOND FLOWERS

MAKES 12 TO 16 FLOWERS, DEPENDING ON FONDANT CUTTER SIZE, OR SIZE YOU WANT TO MAKE THEM

Confectioners' sugar
¼ cup marzipan (comes in tube, usu-
    ally in the baking aisle. Check
    ingredients to make sure it's vegan
    and does not contain egg whites)
Very small drop red food coloring,
    liquid or paste
Dragées (tiny silver or gold sugar
    balls.)

DIRECTIONS

1. Keep a small bowl of confectioners' sugar handy near your workspace. Knead marzipan with a drop of red food coloring; if it gets too sticky, dip fingers in a little powdered sugar. When color is incorporated, dust a smooth surface with a little confectioners' sugar. Pat out dough to a thin even round, and cut out small flour shapes or just form individual petals and press together into flower shapes (we usually make them this way). We like to use a toothpick to press little accent lines onto the petals.

ORANGE PUDDING CUPCAKES
with *Chocolate Ganache*

MAKES 12 CUPCAKES

CITRUS LOVERS WILL be thrilled to pieces over this luscious cake. We cannot resist the chocolate-orange combo, but you can also make a CREAMSICLE CUPCAKE by using ORANGE BUTTERCREAM FROSTING (page 145), or you can skip the filling and add cup of chocolate chips instead.

Prepare the pudding two hours before you make the cupcakes. You can even make it a day ahead, but you will need to stir the pudding before piping it into the cake. Prepare the ganache right before assembling the cupcakes; it needs to be warm and melty.

INGREDIENTS

For the orange pudding filling:
- ¾ cup plain soy milk
- ½ cup freshly squeezed orange juice
- 3 tablespoons tapioca flour, cornstarch, or arrowroot
- ¼ cup plus 2 tablespoons granulated sugar
- 1 teaspoon vanilla extract
- ⅛ teaspoon turmeric for color, optional
- 1 teaspoon finely grated orange zest

For the cupcakes:
- ⅓ cup canola oil
- ¾ cup granulated sugar
- ¾ cup plain soy milk or rice milk
- ½ cup freshly squeezed orange juice
- 1 teaspoon vanilla extract

- 1⅓ cups all-purpose flour
- 1 teaspoon baking powder
- ½ teaspoon baking soda
- ¼ teaspoon salt
- 1 tablespoon finely grated orange zest

For the topping:
- ⅓ cup orange marmalade
- RICH CHOCOLATE GANACHE TOPPING (page 143)

DIRECTIONS

TO MAKE THE PUDDING:

1. Whisk together the soy milk, orange juice, tapioca flour, sugar, vanilla, and turmeric, if using, in a small, heavy-bottomed saucepan.

Cook over medium heat for about 2 minutes until the mixture is warm and steamy, whisking occasionally. When the mixture is warm, you will need to reduce the heat to low and stir continuously for 5 minutes, as the mixture thickens. Use a fork at this point instead of a whisk because the pudding will be too thick for one. When mixture is sufficiently thick and puddinglike, turn the heat off and fold in the orange zest, mixing for another minute.

2. Transfer pudding to a bowl and let cool off the stove for 10 minutes (until it stops steaming). Cover and refrigerate for at least an hour. It will continue to thicken as it cools.

TO MAKE THE CUPCAKES:

1. Preheat oven to 350°F. Line a muffin pan with cupcake liners.
2. In a large bowl, combine the oil, sugar, milk, juice, and vanilla, plus 1 tablespoon of the flour (this will help to emulsify the liquid ingredients), and mix until combined.

3. In a separate bowl sift together remaining flour, baking powder, baking soda, and salt. Add the dry ingredients to the wet ingredients in three batches, mixing well after each addition, until smooth. Fold in the orange zest and mix to distribute.
4. Fill each cupcake liner two-thirds of the way. Bake for 20 to 22 minutes; the tops should spring back when touched.
5. Cool completely before filling with pudding.

TO ASSEMBLE:

1. You will need ⅓ cup orange marmalade that has been stirred with a fork for a spreadable consistency.
2. Fit a pastry bag with a wide piping tip (the widest you can find; if you have trouble piping the pudding through, try cutting the tip). Fill the bag with pudding (depending on the size of the bag you are using you may not be able to get all of the pudding in—just use common sense).

3. Use a finger to poke holes in the top of each cupcake. Fill each cupcake with as much pudding as you can. Use your finger or a knife to remove any excess pudding from the tops of the cupcakes.

4. Place about a teaspoon of marmalade on top of each cupcake. Spread the marmalade into a thin layer.

5. Spoon about 1 tablespoon of RICH CHOCOLATE GANACHE TOPPING onto each cupcake. Use the back of a spoon or a palette knife and gently spread the ganache over the marmalade (try not to get the two mixed up—though no big deal if you do, just try your best.)

6. Place the cupcakes in the fridge to set the ganache. An easy way to do this is put them all on a cutting board and place the whole thing on a shelf.

7. If you feel inspired, decorate by placing candied orange peels in the still wet ganache before placing in the fridge. Alternatively, place a thin slice of orange (without the peel) in the soft ganache.

MEXICAN HOT CHOCOLATE CUPCAKES

MAKES 12 CUPCAKES

OUR FAVORITE WARM and toasty drink made into a cupcake-able form. These have a subtle, crunchy top and a very moist interior with a delicate crumb thanks to the addition of coconut milk. The corn flour and almonds give it an interesting texture that's a lot like the drink (Mexican hot chocolate has little pleasantly gritty bits in it), and just a little bit of cayenne gives it a spicy kick. Go ahead and make them more spicy, or leave it out altogether and keep them gringo. . . either way they're great.

We like to top these with a simple sifting of confectioners' sugar, cinnamon, and cocoa, but these also are great with CHOCOLATE MOUSSE TOPPING (page 155) or spread with RICH CHOCOLATE GANACHE TOPPING (page 143).

INGREDIENTS

- 1 cup coconut milk
- 1 tablespoon ground flaxseeds
- ¾ cup all-purpose flour
- 2 tablespoons corn flour
- ¼ cup almond meal
- ½ cup cocoa powder
- 1 teaspoon baking powder
- ½ teaspoon baking soda
- ¾ teaspoon salt
- 1 teaspoon ground cinnamon
- Pinch ground cayenne pepper (up to ⅛ teaspoon)

- 1 cup granulated sugar
- ⅓ cup canola oil
- 1 teaspoon vanilla extract
- 1 teaspoon almond extract

For topping:

- ½ cup confectioners' sugar
- 2 tablespoons cocoa powder
- ½ teaspoon ground cinnamon

DIRECTIONS

1. Preheat oven to 350°F and line muffin pan with cupcake liners.
2. Whisk together coconut milk and flaxseeds and allow to sit for 10 minutes.
3. In another bowl, sift together all-purpose flour, corn flour, almond meal, cocoa, baking powder, baking soda, salt, cinnamon, and cayenne.
4. Whisk sugar, oil, vanilla, and almond extract into coconut milk mixture. Gently add wet ingredients to dry. Fill cupcake liners three-quarters of the way. Bake for 22 to 25 minutes until a knife or toothpick inserted through the center of one comes out clean. Transfer to a cooling rack to cool completely.

TO ASSEMBLE:

1. Sift a layer of confectioners' sugar onto the tops of the cooled cakes. Then sift on cocoa (looks best if you concentrate the cocoa toward the center of the cake), then lastly sift on a layer of cinnamon.

Variations:

Top with CHOCOLATE MOUSSE TOPPING (page 155) and add to the mousse 1 teaspoon almond extract and ¼ teaspoon cinnamon. Don't pile too much mousse on these cupcakes as the tops are rather delicate and could cave in a little. But then again, chocolate mousse is worth a little cave-in every now and then.

Sprinkles

We use corn flour in this recipe because it's more finely ground than cornmeal. Use regular cornmeal if you prefer; just avoid anything too grainy or chunky. Some of our testers used masa harina flour with good results as well.

Coconut Lime Cupcakes

COCONUT LIME CUPCAKES

MAKES 12 CUPCAKES

THESE ARE SWEET, tangy, and tropical. It doesn't hurt that they look downright adorable with relatively small effort.

INGREDIENTS

⅓ cup coconut oil
¾ cup granulated sugar
1 cup coconut milk
¼ cup soy milk
1 teaspoon vanilla extract
1 teaspoon coconut extract
1 tablespoon lightly packed finely grated lime zest
1 cup all-purpose flour
½ teaspoon baking soda
½ teaspoon baking powder
¼ teaspoon salt
1 cup unsweetened coconut
LIME BUTTERCREAM ICING (recipe below)
1½ cups unsweetened flaked coconut
Thinly sliced limes, cut in half and then cut up to the peel

DIRECTIONS

1. Preheat oven to 350°F. Line a cupcake pan with liners.
2. Melt the coconut oil in a small saucepan over very low heat. Once melted, turn the heat off but leave it in the pan on the stove so that it stays warm and does not solidify.
3. In a medium bowl, mix together the melted coconut oil and sugar. Add the coconut milk, soy milk, vanilla, coconut extract, and lime zest. Mix to combine.
4. Add the flour, baking soda, baking powder, and salt. Mix until smooth. Add the coconut and mix to incorporate.
5. Bake for 23 to 25 minutes, until the cupcake top springs back when

touched and a toothpick inserted through the center comes out clean.

6. Cool completely before icing.

TO ASSEMBLE:

1. Heap the frosting onto the cupcakes. Place the flaked coconut on a pie plate. Gently roll the cupcakes, sides first, in the coconut. Place decorative lime slices on top. Keep refrigerated until ready to serve.

Sprinkles

You will need 3 limes to get enough zest and juice.

★ ★ ★

LIME BUTTERCREAM FROSTING

½ cup nonhydrogenated shortening
½ cup nonhydrogenated margarine (we use Earth Balance)
3½ cups confectioners' sugar
1 teaspoons vanilla extract
¼ cup fresh lime juice
1 teaspoon finely grated lime zest

DIRECTIONS

1. Beat the shortening and margarine together until combined well and fluffy. Add the sugar and beat for about 3 more minutes. Add the vanilla and lime juice, beat for another 5 to 7 minutes or so until fluffy. Add the zest and mix to distribute. Chill until ready to use.

CHAI LATTE CUPCAKES

MAKES 12 CUPCAKES

WE LOVE DRINKING spiced chai tea with steamed soy milk, but holding a steaming hot latte isn't always the most convenient thing when you need to drive or walk somewhere fast. Plus, you'd have a hard time bringing a dozen of them anywhere. So we give you a light, moist, spicy little vegan cupcake that's just as sublime as the drink. These are rather innocent as cupcakes go, topped with sugar and spices and made with slightly less oil than most cupcakes.

INGREDIENTS

- 1 cup soy milk or rice milk
- 4 black tea bags or 2 tablespoons loose black tea
- ¼ cup canola oil
- ½ cup vanilla or plain soy yogurt
- ¾ cup granulated sugar
- 1 teaspoon vanilla extract
- 1⅓ cups all-purpose flour
- ¼ teaspoon baking soda
- ½ teaspoon baking powder
- ½ teaspoon salt
- 2 teaspoons ground cinnamon
- 1 teaspoon ground cardamom
- ½ teaspoon ground ginger
- ¼ teaspoon ground cloves
- Pinch to ⅛ teaspoon ground white or black pepper

For topping:
- ½ cup confectioners' sugar
- 2 tablespoons cocoa powder
- 1 teaspoon ground cinnamon
- ¼ teaspoon ground nutmeg or ground mace

DIRECTIONS

1. Preheat oven to 350°F and line muffin pan with cupcake liners.
2. Heat soy milk in a small saucepan over medium till almost boiling. Add tea bags, cover, and remove from heat. Let sit for 10 minutes. When ready, dunk teabags a few times in soy milk and squeeze

gently to extract any soy milk before removing. Discard tea bags. Measure the soy milk and tea mixture and add more soy milk if it is less than 1 cup.

3. In a large bowl, whisk together oil, yogurt, sugar, vanilla, and tea mixture until all yogurt lumps disappear. Sift flour, baking powder, baking soda, salt, cinnamon, cardamom, ginger, cloves, and pepper into wet ingredients. Mix until large lumps disappear; some small lumps are okay. Fill tins full and bake about 20 to 22 minutes until a sharp knife inserted comes out clean.

4. Make sure cupcakes are completely cool before adding topping, or sugar will melt and not look pretty and powdery.

TO ASSEMBLE:

1. If desired, prepare a stencil (see page 27) and use the decorating technique described to make pretty designs on the top of cupcakes. Or you can just go ahead and sprinkle it on anarchy-style. Either way, sift confectioners' sugar over cooled cakes first. Then mix together cocoa, cinnamon, and nutmeg in a small bowl. Sift mixture onto each cupcake with or without stencil. Enjoy but don't wear black when eating these babies!

✳ *Sprinkles* ✳

◆ Prevent moisture from soaking into the confectioners' sugar by pre-dusting the tops with additional confectioners' sugar. Come serving time, dust with another layer of sugar, then top with spices and cocoa.

◆ We know that tea snobs will tell us that we're not suppose to squeeze those tea bags, but since this will be used for baking, not drinking, any extra bitterness will be counteracted by all the other things in the recipe.

Variations:

THE EARL OF GREY CUPCAKES: Substitute Earl Grey tea for plain black tea. Omit spices and add ½ teaspoon each grated lemon and orange zest. Leave out spices from topping, dusting with powdered sugar or a thin layer of SUPER NATURAL AGAVE ICING (page 149)

Hazelnut Cupcakes with
Mocha Hazelnut
Mousse Filling

HAZELNUT CUPCAKES
with *Mocha Hazelnut Mousse Filling*

MAKES 12 CUPCAKES

WE WANT TO say these cupcakes are totally European with all these hazelnuts, mocha mousse filling, and dark chocolate. So much so that you'll need to eat these wearing a black turtleneck and driving a tiny but amazingly fuel-efficient car, but who are we kidding. . . they're just really yummy. The filling recipe is a variation of the CHOCOLATE MOUSSE TOPPING and it makes more than you'll be able to stuff into twelve cupcakes. But since when did people start complaining about a little leftover chocolate mocha mousse? Use it for dessert the next day.

P.S.: We know you love your chocolate but please check out the raspberry-filled LINZER TORTE variation just once. Trust us.

INGREDIENTS

1 cup plus 2 tablespoons all-purpose flour
⅓ cup hazelnut meal or hazelnut flour
1 teaspoon baking powder
¼ teaspoon baking soda
½ teaspoon ground cinnamon
¼ teaspoon ground nutmeg
½ teaspoon salt
⅔ cup rice milk or nut milk
1 tablespoon ground flaxseeds
⅓ cup canola oil
¼ cup maple syrup
½ cup brown sugar, packed
1 teaspoon vanilla extract
1 tablespoon hazelnut liqueur, or 1½
   teaspoons hazelnut extract

RICH CHOCOLATE GANACHE TOPPING
(page 143)
1 cup chopped toasted hazelnuts, for
   garnish

DIRECTIONS

1. Make the MOCHA HAZELNUT MOUSSE FILLING (recipe below) first and prepare the RICH CHOCOLATE GANACHE TOPPING when cupcakes are fully cool.

TO MAKE THE CUPCAKES:

1. Line cupcake pan and preheat oven to 350°F. In a small bowl, whisk

together rice milk and ground flaxseed. In a large bowl, sift together flour, hazelnut meal, baking powder, baking soda, cinnamon, nutmeg, and salt.

2. Add the maple syrup, sugar, canola oil, vanilla, and hazelnut liquor to the rice milk mixture and beat well. Add wet ingredients to dry, mixing till mostly smooth. Pour into liners, filling them two-thirds of the way. Bake 22 to 24 minutes till a toothpick inserted through the center of one comes out clean. Cool completely on racks before filling.

TO ASSEMBLE:

1. Fit a pastry bag with a wide piping tip. Fill the bag with MOCHA HAZELNUT MOUSSE FILLING. Have RICH CHOCOLATE GANACHE TOPPING prepared and a frosting spatula ready for frosting cupcakes.

2. Use a finger to poke holes in the top of each cupcake. Fill each cupcake with as much mousse as you can. Use your finger or a knife to remove any excess cream from the tops of the cupcake. Spread the ganache onto cupcakes—two layers of ganache (a heaping teaspoon each time) can help create a smoother surface. Sprinkle with chopped hazelnuts. Place the cupcakes in the fridge to set the ganache. An easy way to do this is put them all on a cutting board and place the whole thing on a shelf.

❋ *Sprinkles* ❋

✦ The easiest way to toast hazelnuts: preheat oven to 300°F. Place raw hazelnuts on a baking sheet and roast for 12 to 15 minutes till skins are peeling and nuts appear toasted; be careful not to burn them. Remove from oven. While nuts are still hot, pour into the center of a large rough kitchen towel. Twist ends of towel tightly around nuts to form a sack. Agitate sack vigorously for a few minutes to remove skins. Some skin might still stick to hazelnuts, but this is okay. Everything is going to be okay.

✦ Almond meal or ground almonds can be substituted for ground hazelnuts.

★ ★ ★

MOCHA HAZELNUT MOUSSE FILLING

6 ounces extra-firm silken tofu (half a package of the aseptic kind, such as Mori-Nu)
2 tablespoons plain soy milk
1 tablespoon agave nectar or pure maple syrup
4 teaspoons instant espresso powder
2 teaspoons hazelnut liqueur
1 teaspoon vanilla extract
6 ounces semisweet chocolate, chopped, or $\frac{2}{3}$ cup semisweet chocolate chips

DIRECTIONS

1. Crumble the tofu into a blender. Add the soy milk, agave nectar or maple syrup, espresso powder, hazelnut liqueur, and vanilla. Puree until completely smooth. Set aside.

2. In a double boiler, melt the chocolate chips. Obviously you don't have a double boiler, so take a small saucepan and fill halfway with water. On top of that place a small sauté pan. Fill the sauté pan with chocolate chips and bring the water to a boil. Use a rubber spatula to mix the chocolate as it melts. Once melted, remove from heat and let cool for 5 more minutes, stirring occasionally.

3. Add the chocolate to the tofu and blend until combined, using the spatula to scrape down the sides of the blender every so often.

4. Transfer the mousse to an airtight container or a bowl covered in plastic wrap. Let chill for an hour to firm. Remove from the refrigerator 10 minutes before you are ready to use it. Stir with a fork if it is too firm to work with.

Variation:

LINZER TORTE CUPCAKES: Omit Mocha Hazelnut Mousse Filling, instead using raspberry preserves (about $\frac{2}{3}$ cup should do). Fill cupcakes the same way, brush any remaining preserves on top of cupcakes before topping with RICH CHOCOLATE GANACHE TOPPING and hazelnuts.

Pistachio Rosewater Cupcakes

PISTACHIO ROSEWATER CUPCAKES

MAKES 12 CUPCAKES

A PRETTY, MOIST, and nutty cupcake that we like to think would be the perfect finale to a lavish Persian feast if anyone ever invited us to one. We love the simple rosewater icing that tops these cupcakes, but for something different, whip up a batch of VEGAN FLUFFY BUTTERCREAM FROSTING (page 142) made with an teaspoon of rosewater, and tint it a pretty pink if you're feeling particularly girly.

INGREDIENTS

½ cup vanilla soy yogurt
⅔ cup soy milk or rice milk
⅓ cup canola oil
¾ cup plus 2 tablespoons granulated sugar
1 to 2 tablespoons rosewater
1 cup plus 2 tablespoons all-purpose flour
2 tablespoons cornstarch
½ teaspoon baking powder
½ teaspoon baking soda
¼ teaspoon salt
Generous pinch cardamom
⅓ cup finely chopped pistachios, lightly toasted if desired
ROSEWATER GLAZE (recipe follows)
Chopped pistachios, for garnish (about ½ cup)
Pink decorating sugar crystals, (about 1 tablespoon), optional

DIRECTIONS

1. Preheat oven to 350ºF. Line muffin pan with 12 cupcake liners.

2. In a large mixing bowl, whisk together yogurt, soy milk, oil, sugar, and rosewater. Sift in flour, cornstarch, baking soda, baking powder, cardamom and salt. Mix until relatively smooth. Fold in pistachios. Fill liners three-quarters of the way. Bake 20 to 22 minutes. Transfer to a cooling rack and let cool completely before frosting.

★ ★ ★

ROSEWATER GLAZE

1¼ to 1½ cups powdered sugar,
  sifted
1 tablespoon margarine
2 to 3 teaspoons soy milk
½ teaspoon rosewater

DIRECTIONS

1. With a fork, cream together half of the confectioners' sugar and margarine till mixture resembles fine crumbs. Add in soy milk and rosewater, and beat in remaining confectioners' sugar (you can use an electric mixer, low speed, at this stage). Mixture should have consistency of a thick batter with a satiny sheen. Adjust consistency if needed by beating in small amounts of confectioners' sugar or carefully dribbling in soy milk.

☀ *Sprinkles* ☀

✦ Be sure to use high-quality rosewater made with real roses (check the ingredients to make sure there's no "perfume" or synthetic ingredients and that it's meant for kitchen use). We found our rosewater at a Middle Eastern grocer, but since everyone can't travel to such exciting destinations like Queens, there's always the spice/baking aisle of well-stocked gourmet stores, or try shopping online.

TIRAMISÙ CUPCAKES

IF YOU SERVE these cupcakes on your first date, don't be surprised if your suitor becomes clingy. We suggest playing it cool and serving it on your second or third date. Traditional tiramisù is made by soaking ladyfingers in coffee and Marsala wine, but we prefer the taste that coffee liqueur brings to the party. They can get messy, so serve on a small plate with a cute little fork. You can usually find little forks at a kitchen supply store for under a dollar and it's worth it for moments like this. You can make these a few hours ahead, but they should be served on the same day.

INGREDIENTS

VEGAN CREAM CHEESE FROSTING
(page 158)
GOLDEN VANILLA CUPCAKES, made using
the oil variation (page 33)
⅓ cup espresso or strong coffee
⅓ cup Kahlúa or other coffee-flavored
liqueur
1 tablespoon cocoa powder
¼ teaspoon ground cinnamon
12 chocolate-covered coffee beans, or 12
chocolate chips, or 12 coffee beans

DIRECTIONS

1. Mix together the espresso and the Kahlúa.

2. Use a measuring spoon, a regular teaspoon, or a paring knife to carve out a small cone in the center of the cupcake. Place spoon about 1 inch from the center of the cupcake, then dig the spoon in about 1 inch deep and cut a circle around the center. Carefully scoop out a cone, trying your best to keep the chunk as intact as possible.

3. Use a spoon to pour the Kahlúa mixture in the cavity of the cut cupcake, making sure that all sides of the cavity are drenched, using up to 2 tablespoons of liquid per cup

Tiramisù Cupcakes

cake. Scoop about 2 tablespoons of VEGAN CREAM CHEESE FROSTING into the cavity and smooth over with the back of the spoon. (Make sure to reserve a few tablespoons of frosting to dollop on top of the cupcake). Dip the bottom of the cut-out chunk into the Kahlúa mixture, but keep the top part dry. Place the cut-out chunk on top of the frosting and gently pat it into place. Continue the process with the remaining cupcakes.

4. Place the chocolate and cinnamon a small strainer and dust all of the cupcakes. Dollop a small amount of the frosting on top and place a chocolate chip or espresso bean on the dollop. Let sit for about 10 minutes and serve.

LYCHEE CUPCAKES

with Coconut Glaze

MAKES 12 CUPCAKES

THIS RECIPE COMES from Cheryl Porro, better known to anyone who has ever looked at a cupcake online as Chockylit (www.cupcakeblog.com). We drool over her cupcake blog on a daily basis so we asked her to contribute a recipe. In the world of celebrity cupcake-makers, this is like having the Queen of England offer to catsit for you. Cheryl came up with this sweet and fruity lychee concoction that we love.

INGREDIENTS

2 cups unbleached, all-purpose flour
1½ teaspoons baking powder
½ teaspoon salt
1⅓ cups granulated sugar
5 tablespoons ground flaxseeds
⅓ cup oil
¼ cup coconut milk
1 can (4 ounces) lychee fruit, drained and chopped, syrup reserved
¼ cup lychee syrup
2 teaspoons vanilla extract
COCONUT GLAZE (recipe below)

DIRECTIONS

1. Preheat oven to 350°F. Line a muffin pan with cupcake liners.
2. In a large bowl sift together flour, baking powder, salt, and sugar.
3. In a separate medium bowl, beat ground flaxseeds and 6 tablespoons water with a fork until gelatinous.

Add oil, coconut milk, chopped lychees, and lychee syrup to the flaxseeds and mix to combine.

4. Add wet mixture to the dry ingredients, mix to combine. Fill cupcake liners full. Bake for 22 to 25 minutes or until a toothpick comes out clean.

★ ★ ★

COCONUT GLAZE

2 cups sifted confectioners' sugar
¼ cup coconut milk

DIRECTIONS

1. Mix sifted confectioners' sugar and coconut milk until smooth. Pour over completely cooled cupcakes.

RUM RAISIN CUPCAKES

with *Rum Glaze and Rummy Buttercream Frosting*

MAKES 12 CUPCAKES

BURSTING WITH RUM-SOAKED raisins and topped with a shiny, buttery rum glaze and a rich rum buttercream, these cupcakes are just a little grown-up tasting. They might be a good fit for pirates, because pirates love vegan cupcakes with rum. Vegan pirates that is. And vegan pirate parrots, who love the shoulders of vegan pirates who love rum.

The rum buttercream is very rich and the recipe makes just enough to top these cakes with a small swirl, allowing a little of the shiny glazed tops to show. If you're in a hurry because your ship is being boarded by scurvy dogs and you must escape with an insane yet gorgeous dreadlocked pirate captain wearing eyeliner, skip the frosting and make do with just the glaze.

INGREDIENTS

⅔ cup dark raisins, coarsely chopped
2 tablespoons dark rum
¾ cup plus 2 tablespoons soy milk
1 teaspoon apple cider vinegar
⅓ cup canola oil
¾ cup granulated sugar
1 tablespoon molasses
1 tablespoon rum
1¼ teaspoons vanilla extract
1¼ cups all-purpose flour
2 tablespoons cornstarch
¾ teaspoon baking powder
½ teaspoon baking soda
½ teaspoon salt
¼ teaspoon ground mace or ground nutmeg

DIRECTIONS

1. Preheat oven to 350°F. Line muffin pan with cupcake liners.
2. In a small bowl, combine chopped raisins and dark rum. Toss well to coat raisins and set aside for at least 30 minutes, stirring occasionally. In another measuring cup, whisk

together soy milk and vinegar and set aside a few minutes to curdle.

3. Pour soy milk mixture into a large bowl and whisk in canola oil, sugar, molasses, rum, and vanilla till blended. Sift in flour, cornstarch, baking powder, baking soda, salt, and mace and stir until ingredients are combined. Fold in rum-soaked raisins and fill cupcake liners three-quarters of the way and bake for 18 to 20 minutes till done.

TO ASSEMBLE:

1. While cupcakes are still warm, drizzle warm RUM GLAZE over tops of cakes—a teaspoon at a time—distributing any remaining glaze among cupcakes. When completely cool, decorate tops with a small swirl of RUMMY BUTTERCREAM FROSTING if desired.

★ ★ ★

RUMMY BUTTERCREAM FROSTING

¼ cup margarine, softened to room temperature
1 to 1¼ cup confectioners' sugar, sifted
1 tablespoon rum
½ teaspoon vanilla extract
1 teaspoon molasses, optional
soy milk, as needed

DIRECTIONS

1. Beat margarine, sugar, and rum together with a handheld mixer at low speed until moistened (to avoid confectioners' sugar flying all over the place), then beat at high speed to cream. Stop after a minute to scrape bowl and add vanilla (and molasses if using; adds a little color and flavor). Beat till thick, fluffy and creamy, about 3 to 5 minutes. Add small increments of confectioners' sugar if too wet; dribble in a little soy milk if too dry. Store in refrigerator or load up a pastry bag to decorate cakes with.

Variation:

Add 1 teaspoon of grated orange rind and ¼ teaspoon orange extract to cupcake batter.

Or try substituting half or all of the raisins with finely chopped dates.

Sprinkles

For less mess glazing, move cupcakes to a plate to top with glaze, then return to rack to finish cooling.

★ ★ ★

RUM GLAZE

¼ cup dark rum
3 tablespoons granulated sugar
½ teaspoon vanilla extract
2 teaspoons margarine

DIRECTIONS

1. In a small saucepan, bring rum and sugar to a simmer over medium heat, dissolving sugar and bubbling for about a minute. Reduce heat and cook mixture for another 1 to 2 minutes till it resembles a thin, light-colored syrup. Remove from heat and stir in vanilla and margarine. Allow to cool for a few minutes before dribbling over warm cupcakes.

PUMPKIN CHOCOLATE CHIP CUPCAKES

with Cinnamon Icing

MAKES 12 CUPCAKES

WE LOVE THE taste of pumpkin and chocolate, we didn't spice this up too much so as not to upset this delicate balance. The icing is a tiny amount, piped on to give it a little something something. Just let someone try and call this a muffin.

INGREDIENTS

- 1 cup canned pumpkin
- ⅓ cup oil
- 1 cup granulated sugar
- ¼ cup soy milk
- 1 teaspoon vanilla extract
- 1¼ cups all-purpose flour
- ½ teaspoon baking powder
- ½ teaspoon baking soda
- ½ teaspoon ground cinnamon
- ¼ teaspoon salt
- ½ cup chocolate chips
- CINNAMON ICING (recipe below)

DIRECTIONS

1. Preheat oven to 350°F. Line muffin pan with cupcake liners.
2. In a medium bowl, stir together pumpkin, oil, sugar, soy milk, and vanilla. Sift in the flour, baking

★ ★ ★

CINNAMON ICING

- ½ cup confectioners' sugar
- ½ teaspoon ground cinnamon
- 2 tablespoons margarine, melted
- 1 tablespoon soy milk
- ½ teaspoon vanilla extract

DIRECTIONS

1. Place sugar and cinnamon in a small bowl. Add the margarine, soy milk, and vanilla and stir with a fork until smooth. Keep at room temperature until ready to use. The mixture should look opaque and honey brown. If it's glistening a lot or looks too liquid, add a little extra confectioners' sugar.

powder, baking soda, cinnamon, salt. Stir together with a fork—don't use a handheld mixer, as it will make the batter gummy. Once well combined, fold in the chocolate chips.

3. Fill liners two-thirds full. Bake for 22 to 24 minutes. Transfer to a wire rack and let fully cool before icing.

TO ASSEMBLE:

1. Take a small plastic sandwich bag and cut out a tiny hole in one edge or fit a pastry bag with a small-holed decorating tip. Fill the bag with icing and pipe it out Jackson Pollack-style onto the cupcakes. You may also opt to pipe it in zig-zags, lines, or swirls. Let the icing set at room temperature or refrigerated.

CASHEW BUTTER CARDAMOM CUPCAKES

with *Rich Cashew Butter Frosting*

MAKES 12 CUPCAKES

YOU KNOW WHEN somebody says something obvious about a particular food, like "These cookies are especially for cookie lovers"? These cupcakes are perfect for the extreme cashew butter connoisseur in your life. An exquisitely creamy cashew frosting tops this moist, very tender, and not-too-sweet cake. We'll be the first to admit that they're just a little bit muffin-y, with a hint of orange, making them perfect with afternoon tea or a nourishing midday snack. Or dare we speak the words "breakfast cupcake"?

INGREDIENTS

- ½ cup plus 2 tablespoons soy milk or rice milk
- ¼ cup freshly squeezed orange juice
- 2 teaspoon ground flaxseeds
- ⅓ cup canola oil
- ⅓ cup plus 1 tablespoon granulated sugar
- ⅓ cup brown sugar, packed
- ⅓ cup smooth cashew butter
- 1 cup plus 2 tablespoons all-purpose flour
- ¾ teaspoon baking powder
- ½ teaspoon baking soda
- ½ teaspoon salt
- 1 teaspoon ground cardamom
- ¼ teaspoon ground cinnamon
- 1 teaspoon finely grated orange zest
- RICH CASHEW BUTTER FROSTING (recipe below)

DIRECTIONS

1. Preheat oven to 350°F and line a muffin pan with paper liners.
2. In a large bowl, whisk together soy milk, orange juice, orange zest and flaxseeds until frothy. Add oil, granulated sugar, brown sugar, and cashew butter to soy milk mixture and beat for one minute till frothy.

3. In a separate bowl, sift together flour, baking powder, baking soda, salt, cardamom, and cinnamon.

4. Add dry ingredients to wet in two separate batches, and beat with electric mixer or whisk for about two minutes in total. Fill cupcake liners two-thirds of the way full and bake for 22 to 24 minutes till a toothpick inserted through the center of one comes out clean. Allow to cool completely before frosting.

★ ★ ★

RICH CASHEW BUTTER FROSTING

⅓ cup smooth cashew butter
3 tablespoons margarine, softened
1 teaspoon vanilla extract
½ cup maple syrup
½ teaspoon ground cardamom
½ cup soy milk powder

DIRECTIONS

1. Beat cashew butter and margarine with an electric mixer at low speed till light colored and thick. Beat in vanilla, maple syrup, and cardamom for one minute. Beat in soy milk powder in two batches; frosting will be thick and creamy. Refrigerate for at least 15 minutes before using to help it firm up.

2. Frost cupcakes with a palette knife. This recipe makes a generous amount, so don't be stingy frosting those cupcakes!

Apple Cider Cupcakes

APPLE CIDER CUPCAKES

MAKES 12 CUPCAKES

THIS IS THE quintessential fall cupcake. Prepare the apple cider just as if you were going to drink it, boiled with plenty of whole cinnamon, cloves, and allspice. Top with either VEGAN FLUFFY BUT-TERCREAM FROSTING or SUPER NATURAL AGAVE ICING, and a healthy dose of BROWN RICE CARAMEL GLAZE, and you've got yourself autumn in a yummy little package. The secret ingredient is agar—it gives the cupcakes a bright sheen and holds things together nicely.

INGREDIENTS

- 2 cups apple cider
- 1 tablespoon agar flakes or 1 teaspoon agar powder
- 2 cinnamon sticks
- ½ teaspoon whole cloves
- ½ teaspoon whole allspice
- ½ cup apple butter
- ¼ cup maple syrup
- ¾ cup granulated sugar
- ⅓ cup vegetable oil
- 2 teaspoons apple cider vinegar
- 1 teaspoon vanilla extract
- 1⅓ cups all-purpose flour
- ½ teaspoon baking powder
- 1 teaspoon baking soda
- ¼ teaspoon salt
- VEGAN FLUFFY BUTTERCREAM FROSTING (page 142) or SUPER NATURAL AGAVE ICING (page 149)
- CARAMEL BROWN RICE GLAZE (page 146), optional
- Cinnamon sugar or ground cinnamon for sprinkling

DIRECTIONS

1. Preheat the oven to 350°F . Line a muffin tray with cupcake liners.
2. Place apple cider, agar agar, cinnamon sticks, cloves and allspice in a small saucepan. If using agar flakes, let mixture soak for 10 minutes; if using powder, proceed to the next step.

3. Sift together flour, baking powder, baking soda and salt.

4. In a separate bowl, mix together the apple butter, maple syrup, sugar, vegetable oil, apple cider vinegar and vanilla.

5. Bring the apple cider mixture to a boil, then lower heat to bring it to a low rolling boil, careful not to let it boil over. Boil for about 15 minutes, until the cider is reduced to 1¼ cups and the agar agar is dissolved. (If the cider hasn't reduced enough, boil longer. If it has reduced too much, add extra apple cider to make up for the difference.) Stir frequently because the agar agar tends to stick to the sides of the pan.

6. Strain the apple cider and discard the spices. Let cool to lukewarm, then add the apple cider to the apple butter mixture and mix well. Add the flour mixture to the wet ingredients in roughly three batches, mixing well after each addition.

7. Spray the cupcake liners with non-stick cooking spray. Fill each liner three-quarters full. Bake for 22 to 25 minutes, until a toothpick inserted into the center of a cupcake comes out clean.

8. Transfer to a cooling rack and let cool completely before frosting.

TO ASSEMBLE:

1. Pipe the buttercream or agave icing onto the cupcakes and sprinkle some cinnamon or cinnamon sugar on top of it. Use a spoon to drizzle the caramel over the frosting. It would be cute to stick a cinnamon stick into the frosting if you are feeling fancy-pants.

Sprinkles

The spices called for are in their whole form. If you can't find whole spices, add ¼ teaspoon each ground cinnamon and ground allspice and ⅛ teaspoon ground cloves to the flour mixture.

MUCHO MARGARITA CUPCAKES

MAKES 12 CUPCAKES

THESE CUPCAKES HAVE a lot going for them—lots of fresh lime juice, pretty green lime zest, and even a shot of tequila. But let's get serious. . . it's all about the margarita icing. The pale green frosting has a secret ingredient—kosher salt—that makes each bite sweet, tangy, and savory. If salt in a glaze sounds weird or you like your margaritas sans the salted rim, leave it out today, but make it with the salt for the margarita lover in your life tomorrow. The large crystal sugar that decorates the edges is worth finding; the crunch is a great contrast to the cool, smooth icing.

INGREDIENTS

¼ cup freshly squeezed lime juice
1½ teaspoons finely grated lime zest
1 cup soy milk or rice milk
¼ cup canola oil
2 tablespoons tequila
½ teaspoon vanilla extract
¾ cup granulated sugar
1⅓ cups all-purpose flour
¼ teaspoon baking soda
½ teaspoon baking powder
½ teaspoon salt
Margarita Icing (recipe follows)
Large crystal decorating sugar, for
    decorating edges of cupcakes
    (about ½ cup)

DIRECTIONS

1. Preheat oven to 350°F. Line muffin pan with cupcake liners.

2. In a large bowl, beat together lime juice, zest, soy milk, canola oil, tequila, vanilla, and sugar. Sift in flour, baking soda, baking powder, and salt. Mix until batter is smooth. Fill liners three-quarters of the way full and bake 20 to 22 minutes until a toothpick or knife inserted through the center of one comes out clean. Transfer cupcakes to a cooling rack and let cool completely before frosting; allowing cupcakes

to set for an hour or two helps the flavor to develop fully.

TO ASSEMBLE:

1. Spread icing on cupcakes, spreading all the way to the edges, then roll just the outer edges of cupcake in sugar crystals. If this is way too messy, just sprinkle sugar crystals on edges of cupcake by hand.

★ ★ ★

MARGARITA ICING

¼ cup margarine, softened
1 tablespoons soy milk or rice milk
3 tablespoons lime juice
1 tablespoon tequila
tiniest drop of green food color or
    food color paste you can manage,
    optional
2 cups confectioners' sugar, sifted
Generous pinch to ⅛ teaspoon
    kosher or coarse salt, optional

DIRECTIONS

1. Blend margarine with a fork till soft and fluffy, then stir in soy milk, lime juice, tequila, and food coloring if using (the effect is just to give the icing a very pale green tint, even lighter than "mint" green). Sift in 2 cups confectioners' sugar and blend (an electric mixer a low speed helps at this point) till creamy and smooth. If it's a little too liquidy for your taste, sift in the remaining confectioners' sugar, one tablespoon at a time, till a thick but spreadable consistency is reached. Refrigerate till ready to use.

Mucho Margarita Cupcakes

BLUEBERRY LEMON CRÈME CUPCAKES

MAKES 12 CUPCAKES

SUNNY, LEMONY, BLUEBERRY bliss. Another towering, filled cupcake made simple and easy, based on some of our best, never-fail favorite recipes. Serve immediately after assembling and accompany with a tiny spoon for devouring.

INGREDIENTS
LEMONY VANILLA CUPCAKES (page 36)
LEMON BUTTERCREAM (page 96)

DIRECTIONS

1. Prepare LEMON BUTTERCREAM with additional lemon zest and extracts and refrigerate till ready to use.

LUSCIOUS BLUEBERRY COMPOTE

1 (12-ounce) bag frozen blueberries
    (preferably small, wild berries), thawed
2 teaspoons arrowroot
2 tablespoons lemon juice
2 tablespoons granulated sugar

DIRECTIONS

1. Combine thawed blueberries, their juice, arrowroot, lemon juice, and sugar in a saucepan and cook over medium heat. Stir till mixture starts to simmer, about 4 to 5 minutes. Keep stirring, mixture will rapidly thicken. Remove from heat and let cool to room temperature.

TO ASSEMBLE:

1. With a tablespoon (the large kind you eat soup with or measure with) or a paring knife, carefully dig a neat cone out of the top of each cupcake. Set aside the cones.

2. Load buttercream frosting into a pastry bag fitted with a large star or round tip, and keep handy.

3. Spoon a heaping tablespoon of blueberries and sauce into the well of each cupcake, distributing any remaining compote among the cakes. Pipe a small dollop of frosting on top of compote, then gently but firmly replace the cone tops onto the cupcakes. Pipe another dollop of frosting onto cupcake tops, then sprinkle lemon zest or dribble a little remaining blueberry sauce on top. Serve immediately.

CAPPUCCINO CUPCAKES
filled with Espresso Crème

MAKES 12 CUPCAKES

MOIST 'N' LIGHT, these cappuccino-flavored cupcakes filled with espresso pastry crème can be as innocent or devious as you like, depending on what you top them with. Keep it simple by topping with a little sifted confectioners' sugar and cocoa powder, and pipe a little rosette of more espresso crème in the center. Get decadent by spreading on the RICH CHOCOLATE GANACHE TOPPING (page 143), SUPER NATURAL AGAVE ICING (page 149) sprinkled with cocoa, or VEGAN FLUFFY BUTTERCREAM FROSTING (page 142) flavored with coffee extract, drizzled with QUICK MELTY GANACHE (page 160) and dusted with cocoa powder. Prepare the pastry crème (recipe follows) before the cupcakes because it needs some time to set.

INGREDIENTS

⅓ cup canola oil
¾ cup granulated sugar
½ cup vanilla soy yogurt
⅔ cup soy or rice milk
1 teaspoon vanilla extract
2–3 tablespoons instant espresso powder
1¼ cups all-purpose flour
1 tablespoon unsweetened cocoa powder
1 teaspoon baking powder
¼ teaspoon baking soda
½ teaspoon ground cinnamon
½ teaspoon salt
CAPPUCCINO PASTRY CRÈME
   (recipe follows)

DIRECTIONS

1. Preheat oven to 350°F. Line muffin pan with paper liners.

2. In a large bowl, whisk together oil, sugar, yogurt, soy milk, vanilla, and espresso powder till smooth. Sift in flour, cocoa, baking powder, baking soda, cinnamon, and salt. Mix until combined and smooth.

3. Fill liners three-quarters full and bake for 20 to 22 minutes. These cupcakes are best when not over-baked. It's okay if the tester tooth-pick has a few moist crumbs stuck

★ ★ ★

ESPRESSO PASTRY CRÈME

½ cup soy milk
1 teaspoon powdered agar or 1½ tablespoons agar flakes
4 teaspoons arrowroot
6 ounces extra-firm silken tofu (half an aseptic package,
    such as Mori-Nu), drained
⅓ cup granulated sugar
1 tablespoon espresso powder
1 teaspoon vanilla extract
Pinch salt

DIRECTIONS

1. Pour ⅓ cup of the soy milk into a small saucepan; keep the remaining soy milk in the measuring cup. Add agar powder to the saucepan and cook mixture over medium heat, stirring constantly. Bring mixture to a boil, reduce heat, and continue to cook the mixture till agar is dissolved, about 4 minutes.

2. Whisk arrowroot into the remaining soy milk. Pour arrowroot mixture in a steady stream into agar mixture, stirring the whole time. The mixture will cook and get very thick in 1 minute or less; when done it will resemble a very thick pudding. Remove from heat and set aside.

3. Crumble tofu into a blender, add espresso powder, sugar, salt, and cooked arrowroot mixture. Blend till creamy. Scrape sides of blender, add vanilla, and blend again. Scrape mixture into a covered container and put in refrigerator to chill and firm up, at least 40 minutes.

to it. Transfer to cooling racks to cool completely before filling and frosting.

TO ASSEMBLE:

1. Poke each cupcake in the center, almost to the bottom, to create a hole for the filling. Very gently, press the sides and bottom of the hole to widen it; you'll want the extra little space to be able to fill it in with lots of custard.

2. Fit a pastry bag with a large round or star-tipped nozzle and fill with CAPPUCCINO PASTRY CRÈME. Fill only halfway to make handling the bag easier. Pipe pastry crème into each cupcake, trying to get as much filling as possible into cakes. Cupcakes should feel noticeably heavier. Remove any excess crème on top by wiping with a knife or finger. Frost or top as desired.

✳ *Sprinkles* ✳

✦ Regular instant coffee can be substituted for espresso powder.

✦ If you use agar flakes, you will need to soak the flakes in the soy milk for 10 minutes first. The cooking time will also be longer, about 4 to 6 minutes. Stir constantly, to melt any stray flakes that stick to the sides of the pan and watch very carefully so as to not burn the soy milk.

FROSTIN'S AND FILLIN'S

YOUR CUPCAKE IS only half a cupcake without the proper frosting or topping. We say go the extra mile, or even a few inches, and make that cupcake beyond fabulous with the addition of a creamy, chocolaty, or fruity filling.

VEGAN FLUFFY BUTTERCREAM FROSTING

THIS IS OUR all-purpose "go to" frosting. It's great for piping into lush, swirling mountains of frostiness and just as good for spreading onto a cupcake like rolling hills of heaven. It makes a lot, probably 4 cups' worth, so you can halve the recipe if you are going to be spreading the frosting rather than piping it.

INGREDIENTS

- ½ cup nonhydrogenated shortening
- ½ cup nonhydrogenated margarine (we use Earth Balance)
- 3½ cups confectioners' sugar, sifted if clumpy
- 1½ teaspoons vanilla extract
- ¼ cup plain soy milk or soy creamer

DIRECTIONS

1. Beat the shortening and margarine together until well combined and fluffy. Add the sugar and beat for about 3 more minutes. Add the vanilla and soy milk, beat for another 5 to 7 minutes until fluffy.

RICH CHOCOLATE GANACHE TOPPING
(That We Use for Everything)

LIKE THE NAME says, this is an all-purpose, thick, extreme chocolate glaze that goes with cupcakes of every stripe. Use either vegan semisweet chocolate or any vegan dark chocolate with a cacao content of up to 60 percent.

INGREDIENTS

¼ cup soy milk

4 ounces semisweet chocolate, chopped

2 tablespoons pure maple syrup

DIRECTIONS

1. Bring the soy milk to a gentle boil in a small sauce pan. Immediately remove from heat and add the chocolate and maple syrup. Use a rubber heatproof spatula to mix the chocolate until it is fully melted and smooth. Set aside at room temperature till ready to use.

✳ Sprinkles ✳

◆ Got leftover ganache? Make some mini-truffles to put on some cupcakes! Place leftover ganache in the refrigerator to cool and get very firm. Have some sifted cocoa powder on hand (less than ¼ cup should do), then roll about ¼ to ½ teaspoon cold ganache into a ball with your fingers. Work quickly as the ganache will begin to melt, and then roll truffle in cocoa powder. Set aside finished truffles on wax paper and chill some more to firm up again before topping cupcakes, and keep cool until ready to eat. Especially delish when paired with fresh raspberries or strawberries.

CHOCOLATE BUTTERCREAM FROSTING

FLUFFY. CHOCOLATY. BUTTERCREAMY. Spread or pipe on chocolate or vanilla cupcakes for birthday cupcake perfection.

INGREDIENTS

- ¼ cup margarine, softened
- ¼ cup shortening
- ½ cup unsweetened cocoa powder (sifted if there are clumps)
- 2½ cups powdered sugar, sifted
- 3 tablespoons soymilk
- 1½ teaspoons pure vanilla extract

DIRECTIONS

1. Cream together the margarine and the shortening until well combined. Add the cocoa powder and incorporate well. Add the confectioners sugar in about ½ cup batches and beat well, adding a little splash of soymilk after each addition. When all ingredients have been well incorporated, add the vanilla and beat until light and fluffy (about 3 minutes with a hand mixer, 7 minutes if mixing with a fork).

Variations:

Add a teaspoon of coffee extract for mocha buttercream.

★ ★ ★

ORANGE BUTTERCREAM FROSTING

¼ cup shortening
¼ cup margarine, softened
2 cups confectioners' sugar
2 tablespoons fresh orange juice
1 tablespoon finely grated lemon zest
1 teaspoon vanilla extract

DIRECTIONS

1. In a small bowl, cream the shortening and margarine until well combined. Add the confectioners' sugar in roughly ½-cup additions. After each addition of sugar, add a splash of orange juice and beat well with a handheld mixer on medium speed. Add vanilla and beat for another 3 to 5 minutes until smooth, creamy, and fluffy. Wrap tightly with plastic wrap and refrigerate until ready to use.

BROWN RICE CARAMEL GLAZE

A VERY THICK glaze with a bold, caramel-like flavor, this is an interesting way to use brown rice syrup in desserts. The intense flavor goes perfectly with spice or any strongly flavored cupcake, and is also the basis for our DULCE SIN LECHE CUPCAKES (page 93). The texture of this glaze is very sticky at first but it will set up nicely after an hour, or pop finished cupcakes in the fridge to speed it up.

INGREDIENTS

- ½ cup full-fat soy milk
- ¼ cup soy milk powder
- 1 tablespoon arrowroot
- ½ cup brown rice syrup
- 1 teaspoon vanilla extract

DIRECTIONS

1. In a small saucepan, whisk together soy milk, soy milk powder, and arrowroot. Stir constantly over medium heat till arrowroot is cooked and mixture starts to thicken, about 4 minutes. Stir in brown rice syrup, turn up heat to medium high and bring to a gentle boil, then bring heat back down so mixture is at a low simmer, all the while stirring constantly. Cook till mixture is thick and slightly reduced, about 10 minutes. Sauce will have a thick consistency, like cake batter. Whisk in vanilla and remove from heat.

2. Allow to cool 10 minutes before spreading on warm cupcakes.

Sprinkles

To measure sticky brown rice syrup, lightly spray or rub canola oil on measuring cups. The measured syrup will easily slide right out.

COCONUT PECAN FUDGE FROSTING

A CLASSIC AND simple-to-make cooked icing. Atop YOUR BASIC CHOCOLATE CUPCAKES (page 37) they'll become German chocolate cupcakes. Try spread on any vanilla cupcake variation, too, or make GINGERBREAD CUPCAKES (page 53) extra awesome with this topping.

INGREDIENTS

¼ cup rice milk
2 tablespoons arrowroot or cornstarch
Scant pinch of salt
¾ cup coconut milk
1 cup brown sugar
1½ cups shredded unsweetened coconut
½ cup pecans, coarsely chopped
1 teaspoon vanilla extract
1 tablespoon whiskey or bourbon, optional

DIRECTIONS

1. Whisk rice milk, arrowroot, and salt in a small bowl or measuring cup. In a large stainless-steel saucepan over medium heat, stir together coconut milk and brown sugar. Cook, stirring occasionally, till mixture starts to boil. Turn heat down to low and cook, stirring occasionally, for five minutes. Whisk rice milk mixture once more and slowly pour into the coconut milk mixture, stirring constantly to incorporate.

2. Stir mixture continuously till it darkens again, gets very thick and smooth, and arrowroot is cooked, about 6 to 7 minutes. Remove from heat and beat in vanilla and whiskey, chopped pecans, and coconut. Stir till everything is coated and completely combined. Cool to room temperature before frosting cupcakes.

✳ *Sprinkles* ✳

✦ You can use sweetened coconut in a pinch, the frosting will just be very sweet. Try cutting down the brown sugar by 1 to 3 tablespoons or to taste.

Your Basic Chocolate Cupcake with
Coconut Pecan Fudge Frosting

SUPER NATURAL AGAVE ICING

WE'VE LONG BEEN on a quest for a cupcake topping that's a departure from the usual margarine/shortening/sugar route. Not that those don't have a special place in our hearts, but here's an excuse to use agave nectar the way nature intended (sort of).

This icing isn't haunted and it can't read your mind. . . it's just sweetened naturally with agave nectar and gets its smooth, rich texture from nonhydrogenated coconut oil (sometimes called coconut butter) instead of more refined fats. It's also rather sensitive to heat, so be sure that cupcakes are completely cool before frosting and store iced cupcakes in the fridge until ready to serve.

INGREDIENTS

- ⅓ cup plain soy or rice milk
- 1 tablespoon arrowroot
- Pinch of salt (scant ⅛ teaspoon)
- ⅓ cup light agave nectar
- ⅓ cup refined, nonhydrogenated coconut oil
- 1½ teaspoons vanilla extract
- ½ cup plus 2 tablespoons plain soy milk powder

DIRECTIONS

1. In a small saucepan whisk together rice milk, arrowroot, and salt till dissolved. Cook over medium heat, stirring constantly with a wire whisk, till mixture thickens into a puddinglike consistency, about 2 to 3 minutes. Remove from heat and scrape mixture into a medium-size bowl with a heatproof spatula.

2. Add agave nectar and whisk till combined, then add coconut oil and vanilla extract and whisk again. Add soy milk powder and beat on medium speed with an electric mixer for 4 to 5 minutes, until creamy and smooth. Cover and chill in the refrigerator for at least 40 minutes until mixture is firm, or for best results, allow to chill overnight.

Variations:

Add an additional 1 teaspoon of the following extracts: lemon, strawberry, banana, almond, orange.

COCONUT AGAVE NECTAR ICING: To chilled icing, fold in ½ cup unsweetened shredded coconut. Try making this with unrefined coconut oil for maximum coconut effect!

✳ *Sprinkles* ✳

◆ We like refined coconut oil for this icing. It's nonhydrogenated but has a neutral taste that pairs well with anything that vanilla frosting may tread.

◆ This icing can't be piped on with a pastry bag. It's meant more as a creamy topping to be spooned on or lavished on top of a cupcake with a frosting knife. This also is good drizzled when slightly warm on room temperature bundt cakes or sticky cinnamon buns.

◆ This icing is best flavored with vanilla, fruity, or nutty flavors. For a decadent chocolate icing sweetened with agave nectar, go to the THICK CHOCOLATE FUDGEY FROSTIN' recipe (page 161).

PEANUT BUTTERCREAM
Frosting or Filling

WE'RE IN LOVE with this perfectly light, creamy, and just-right peanut-buttery-tasting buttercream. You'll be, too, when you make this but we won't be the least bit jealous. Use the most creamy, natural peanut butter you can find; try to avoid chunkier varieties where the oil separates easily, instead choose peanut butters whose texture is thinner and the oil seems to stay put better. Also, salted peanut butter gives it a true peanut butter flavor.

The barley malt or molasses is entirely optional; the malty flavor adds even more depth to the roasted taste of peanut butter. But the frosting still tastes great without it.

This recipe makes a generous amount of filling to be piped into cupcakes. Double the amount to frost the top of cupcakes.

INGREDIENTS

¼ cup margarine, softened

2 tablespoons shortening (Earth Balance sticks are the best for this)

⅓ cup creamy peanut butter

1 tablespoon barley malt syrup or molasses, optional

1½ teaspoons vanilla extract

1¼ cups confectioners' sugar, sifted

1 to 2 tablespoons rice milk, soy milk, or soy creamer

DIRECTIONS

1. With electric handheld mixer, cream together margarine and shortening at medium speed till smooth. Add peanut butter, barley malt syrup, and vanilla, and beat until very smooth, 2 to 3 minutes. Beat in sugar; mixture will be very stiff. Dribble in rice milk a little at a time, beating continuously till frosting is pale tan and very fluffy.

Adjust the thickness of the frosting by adding rice milk or more confectioners' sugar in small increments if necessary. Frost or fill cooled cupcakes.

Sprinkles

If using unsalted peanut butter, include a pinch of salt.

NOT-TOO-SWEET BLUEBERRY MOUSSE
Topping or Filling

A CREAMY, SHOCKINGLY purple, and low-fat alternative to many frostings. Probably healthy, too, since it's chock-full of antioxidant-rich berries. It's not the sweetest topping out there, but we like it that way. Cupcakes filled or topped with this should be served within a few hours since this moist topping can make them soggy. We like it especially with The SEXY LOW-FAT VANILLA CUPCAKES (page 41) or SIMPLE VANILLA AND AGAVE NECTAR CUPCAKES (page 44).

INGREDIENTS

- 1 cup frozen blueberries, at room temperature (measure before thawing)
- 6 ounces (about half a box) firm or extra-firm silken aseptic-pack tofu, such as Mori-Nu, drained of any excess liquid
- Dash of salt
- 3 tablespoons agave nectar or maple syrup
- 1 teaspoon lemon juice
- ¼ teaspoon lemon extract, optional
- ⅓ cup water or fruit juice, as needed
- 1 teaspoon agar powder
- 1 tablespoon arrowroot

DIRECTIONS

1. Gently strain juice away from berries and measure; you'll need approximately ⅓ cup of juice. If more liquid is needed, use water or a complementary fruit juice.

2. Blend drained berries, tofu, salt, agave, lemon juice, and lemon extract in a food processor till creamy, 30 to 60 seconds.

3. In a cup, stir together 1 tablespoon of the blueberry juice and the arrowroot and set aside.

4. In a small saucepan, whisk together remaining juice and the agar powder. Bring to a boil over medium-low heat and simmer for about 30

seconds, stirring occasionally, then reduce heat slightly. Pour in the arrowroot mixture in a steady stream and stir constantly till mixture becomes very thick and is no longer opaque, about 1 minute. Remove from heat and with a heatproof spatula pour the mixture into the food processor with tofu mixture. Blend till creamy, scraping the sides of the bowl a few times. Scrape mousse into a container, cover, and put in refrigerator to set, 1 to 2 hours. Whip slightly with a whisk or fork before loading into a pastry bag for piping.

Variation

RASPBERRY MOUSSE OR TOPPING: Substitute frozen raspberries for blueberries. Press thawed raspberries through a strainer to remove seeds. Measure juice and proceed as directed.

Sprinkles

Small "wild" blueberries work best for this recipe. Though agar sets quickly, the flavors in this mousse develop best if allowed to sit overnight.

CHOCOLATE MOUSSE TOPPING

YOU'LL DEFINITELY NEED to break out the pastry bag because this mousse likes to be fancy. Even though it has tofu, this topping is so luscious and rich, it is safe to serve to omnivores. They honestly will never know.

INGREDIENTS

- 1 (12.3-ounce) package extra-firm silken aseptic tofu, such as Mori-Nu, drained of excess liquid
- ¼ cup plain soy milk
- 2 tablespoons agave syrup or maple syrup
- 1 teaspoon vanilla extract
- 1 (12-ounce) package semisweet chocolate chips

DIRECTIONS

1. Crumble the tofu into a blender. Add the soy milk, agave, and vanilla. Puree until completely smooth. Set aside.

2. In a double boiler, melt the chocolate chips. Obviously you don't have a double boiler so take a small saucepan and fill halfway with water. On top of that place a small sauté pan or metal bowl. Fill the sauté pan with chocolate chips and bring the water to a boil. Use a rubber spatula to mix the chocolate as it melts. Once melted, remove from heat and let cool for 5 more minutes, stirring occasionally.

3. Add the chocolate to the tofu and blend until combined, use the spatula to scrape down the sides of the blender every so often.

4. Transfer the mousse to an airtight container or a bowl covered with plastic wrap. Chill for an hour.

**Your Basic Chocolate Cupcake with
Chocolate Mousse Topping**

Variations

CHOCOLATE ORANGE MOUSSE: Replace 2 tablespoons of the soy milk with orange liqueur. Add a teaspoon of finely grated orange zest to the blended tofu.

MOCHA MOUSSE: Add 2 teaspoons coffee extract to the blended tofu or add 1 tablespoon instant coffee to the soy milk and heat until dissolved.

CHOCOLATE BANANA MOUSSE: Add a very ripe banana to the blended tofu.

VEGAN CREAM CHEESE FROSTING

INGREDIENTS

¼ cup nonhydrogenated margarine, softened

¼ cup vegan cream cheese, softened

2 cups confectioners' sugar

1 teaspoon vanilla extract

DIRECTIONS

1. Cream together margarine and cream cheese until just combined. Use a handheld mixer to whip while adding the confectioners sugar in ½ cup batches. Mix until smooth and creamy, then mix in the vanilla. Keep tightly covered and refrigerated until ready to use.

Variations

LEMONY CREAM CHEESE FROSTING: Add 1 tablespoon of finely grated lemon zest.

ORANGE CREAM CHEESE FROSTING: Add 1 tablespoon finely grated orange zest.

COFFEE CREAM CHEESE FROSTING: Add 2 teaspoons coffee extract.

TOASTED WALNUT CREAM CHEESE FROSTING: Add ½ teaspoon almond extract. In a heavy-bottomed pan, toast ½ cup walnut halves for 5 minutes over medium heat, tossing occasionally. Set aside to cool. Finely chop the walnuts and fold into the frosting.

CHOCOLATE CREAM CHEESE FROSTING: Melt 4 (1-ounce) squares bittersweet or semisweet chocolate in a double boiler. Add to the margarine and cream cheese mixture and mix until combined, then proceed with the rest of the recipe.

RASPBERRY BUTTERCREAM FROSTING

ANOTHER ONGOING PROJECT at Vegan Cupcake R&D is creating the perfect raspberry buttercream. We've tried fresh raspberries, reductions, preserves (all either not having enough flavor or tasting too much like preserves), and raspberry extract seems to be a little elusive, so in this version raspberry syrup gets the job done. This is the kind of syrup that's used for lattes and Italian sodas, used by baristas everywhere. Avoid any other kinds of syrup, as in stuff for waffles or pancakes. Try to use an "all-natural" brand for best flavor. It also gives the frosting a nice natural-looking mauve tint, but you can always add a drop of red food coloring if that's how you roll. If you do happen to be the proud owner of actual raspberry extract it makes a fine addition to this the recipe as well, as does strawberry extract.

INGREDIENTS

¼ cup nonhydrogenated shortening
¼ cup margarine
1¾ to 2 cups confectioners' sugar
4 tablespoons raspberry syrup
½ teaspoon raspberry extract,
   or strawberry extract, optional
Drop of red food coloring, optional

DIRECTIONS

1. Cream together shortening and margarine till smooth. With a fork or spatula, work in 1½ cups of the confectioners' sugar, forming a crumbly mixture. Beat in syrup till mixture is creamy, then if mixture is too watery or not fluffy enough, beat in additional confectioners' sugar one tablespoon at a time till desired consistency is reached.

QUICK MELTY GANACHE
for Decorating

A SPEEDY WAY to add a touch of tasty decoration to the tops of already frosted cupcakes. Makes enough to drizzle on a dozen cupcakes

INGREDIENTS

3 tablespoons soy creamer or soy milk
⅓ cup semisweet chocolate chips

DIRECTIONS

1. Heat soy creamer in a small saucepan over medium heat till just about to simmer. Remove from heat; add chocolate chips and stir till chocolate is completely melted and creamer is incorporated. Set aside and allow to cool for 10 minutes. With a spatula scoop into a prepared pastry bag or plastic bag with the tip chopped off, or drizzle haphazardly with a fork. QUICK MELTY GANACHE will set when fully cooled.

THICK CHOCOLATE FUDGEY FROSTIN'

THIS FROSTING HAS a velvety texture that reminds us of kids' birthday parties and school bake sales. Not as sweet or intense as chocolate ganache, its flavor and texture would probably be best suited for kids or anyone who prefers a thick, fudge frosting instead of buttercream toppings.

INGREDIENTS

- ½ cup margarine, softened at room temperature (Earth Balance sticks are best for this)
- ½ cup agave syrup, light or dark
- 2 teaspoons vanilla extract
- ⅓ cup regular cocoa powder, sifted
- ½ cup soy milk powder (don't use vanilla or flavored powders that contain large sugar crystals)

DIRECTIONS

1. Beat margarine and agave with an electric mixer at medium speed till smooth. Whisk in vanilla, then slowly fold in cocoa powder (try folding it by hand with a fork first, then use beaters, so cocoa powder doesn't fly everywhere). Slowly beat in soy milk powder at low speed. If mixture seems too firm, drizzle in a little agave, if too watery add a very small amount of soy milk powder.

2. Frosting might get a little too loose when done mixing; just pop it in the refrigerator for 10 minutes to firm up for spreading. Stores well in refrigerator, just allow to warm at room temperature 15 to 20 minutes before spreading on completely cool cupcakes.

Variations

Try adding 1 to 2 tablespoons whiskey, bourbon, or rum. Also great with the addition of 1 to 2 tablepoons of hazelnut liqueur. Adjust with a little more soy milk powder if the consistency is too thin.

ACKNOWLEDGMENTS

CUPCAKE WORLD DOMINATION would not have been possible without our dedicated, talented, and ridiculously good looking team of foot soldiers in the cupcake test kitchen. Thank you so much to all of you! We love you more than words can say, so a cupcake emoticon will have to suffice [|}

Linda Maley
Carrie Lynn Morse
Paula "Igdy" Gross
Terri Kruse
Erica Manney
Michelle Imber
Kittee Burns
Mike Crooker and Liz Bujack
Dolsey
Webly Bowles
Val Head
Rachel "FooFoo" Bavolar
Abby Fosgate

Katharine Foster
Erica Johnson
Kristen Frazer
Amy Sims
Epidiah Ravachol
Steve Calnan
Elissa Stanton
Leah Dieterich
Michiaki Yamada
Rosemary "Squashy" Savoia
Chris Poupart
Miss Jordan Faulds, Esq
Sarah Peltier
Cassondra "Keenie" Herman even though she didn't test cupcakes
Mat Winser
Molly "Not Vulchy" Tanzer
Amy Mekemson
Steven Wade

Many of our testers post pictures of cupcakes on their Web sites, so be sure to check them out!

http://community.livejournal.com/
    vegancooking/
http://supercarrotcake.livejournal.com/
http://vegan-licious.blogspot.com/
http://www.pakupaku.info/
http://letsgetsconed.blogspot.com/
http://veg-in-training.blogspot.com/
http://vegan-licious.blogspot.com/
http://lakitchen.blogspot.com/
http://www.flickr.com/photos/catsgalore/

ISA WOULD ALSO LIKE TO THANK:
Justin Field, for doing his job (putting the cupcake liners into the trays quickly and efficiently) and for doing so many dishes.

Marlene "Mom" Stewart, even though I don't think she helped out on this one, I'm sure she'll come around for the next.

Arthur "Dad" Moskowitz, I think he stopped by once or twice and did a dish or two.

Michelle "Sister" Moskowitz-Brown and the entire Moskowitz-Brown continuum.

Erica Levine, because I owe her $300 and hope she will take a "thank you" instead.

Josh Hooten for making me famous.

Avocado and Fizzle, for adding a little bit of cat hair to everything.

TERRY WOULD LIKE TO THANK:
John Stavropoulos for not letting me eat all the cupcakes.

My Queens gamer posse for eating anything I put in front of them.

Mom and Dad for letting me use the oven before I could reach the spice rack.

ISA AND TERRY WOULD LIKE TO THANK:
Katie McHugh, Peter Jacoby, and Matthew Lore at Marlowe.

Rebecca Bent for the fabulous photos.

Marc Gerald at the Agency Group.

Post Punk Kitchen Web site:
http://www.theppk.com

INDEX

CONTENTS

FOREWORD

By Sara Quin
TEGAN AND SARA

MY GRANDMA WAS a punk chef. I don't know that she would have acknowledged the term, but at heart, she was always breaking the rules and ignoring the instructions of her own recipes (scrawled on sticky index cards). She knew best what the pie crust needed, and not even her own messy scribbling in the margins could convince her otherwise. Yet even with a hip role model like my grandma teaching me the ropes, I always hated to cook.

Then I fell in love with a passionate individual with a crazy hobby for grocery shopping and extravagant dinners. On our first date, I stared in panic at a mound of mango chutney and wondered what the hell to do with it. So I started calling my grandma to ask her for my favorite childhood recipes, which I then wrote down on my own set of index cards. Maybe there was a punk chef in me after all!

One of my earliest memories of cupcakes is from elementary school. Cupcake Day was run by parent volunteers who donated dozens of cupcakes to sell at the bargain price of 25 cents. At recess we would be lined up in the main hallway of my school and then slowly released into the front lobby, where hundreds of cupcakes were displayed on splintered, wooden tables. I still feel anxious when I think about the sweaty quarter in the palm of my hand, waiting to be traded for a single cupcake.

Vegan Cupcakes Take Over the World is my dream come true. The "oohhs" and "aahhs" that my partner and I get when we present Isa Chandra Moskowitz's cupcakes at dinner parties is well worth tying on an apron for. I plan on enjoying each one of the innovative delights found in this book while pretending that they contribute to my healthy lifestyle. Vegans need some indulgence, too! If my grandma were still baking today, I would excitedly send her this collection of cupcake recipes. Even though she might ignore all of the instructions. . . .

INTRODUCTION

WELCOME TO *Vegan Cupcakes Take Over the World*!

Who would think that something as simple and unassuming as a cupcake would bring about the revolution? The world is enraptured with this tiny cake—maybe it's our selfishness, knowing that the cake is "Mine! All mine!" Maybe it's our obsession with beauty; cupcakes, like flowers, seem to have the perfect proportions to capture our eye. Maybe they speak to the child in all of us, our yearning for a simpler time, where a little something sweet was a reminder that there was something to celebrate.

And, vegan cupcakes are the ultimate subversive tool. They can be snuck into the office, birthday parties, bat mitzvahs, the Super Bowl, what have you. Innocent and adorable, no one will suspect that these toothsome morsels are cruelty-free. No one will miss the dairy—and why should they? These cakes taste just as good, and some may argue *even better* than their out-moded counterparts.

We believe in the evolution of dessert. We don't want to be bogged down with the rigmarole of what has been and what will always be. We simply *don't need* dairy and eggs to have sweet, satisfying, and decadent treats. It's time to move on. Have we mentioned that moving on has never tasted so damn good?

This book has been a labor of love for us. We decided to write it for the simple reason that people freak out over our cupcakes. We spent months and months with our dedicated group of testers making sure that they were up to par not only for the vegan palate, but for omnivores as well. Test subjects included cubicle mates, skeptical parents, cab drivers, beefy football guys, kindergarten graduates, grandmothers, D&D nerds . . . they ran the gamut. It was a fun sociological experiment, as sometimes they knew the cupcakes were vegan, other times not. But across the board they were impressed. Our little cupcakes set out on their mission to change the world and they did their job tenfold. *Amor vincit omnia*. Love really does conquer all! Viva la Cupcake!

CUPCAKES A TO Z

WHY CUPCAKES? WE feel that this question can only be answered with an A to Z list.

ADORABLE. This one is obvious. Who doesn't think cupcakes are cute? Off the top of our heads, probably only Dick Cheney.

BLOGWORTHY. A surefire way to get people to look at your blog is by posting pictures of cupcakes. No one wants to hear about your terrible day at the office or what you think of China's space program. They want to see pictures of cupcakes, trust us.

CRAFTY. You can get all creative in the kitchen without the glue or the scrapbook that no one wants to look at.

DELICIOUS. They taste good.

EVERYWHERE. Cupcakes are everywhere. So the logic follows that if cupcakes are everywhere, people must love cupcakes, therefore they will love a book about cupcakes.

FORKS. Fork it, who needs forks? Eat with your hands.

GIFTS. Cupcakes make the best gift! I dare you to give someone a cupcake and have them not smile.

HOME. Baking makes a house a home. Whether, like us, you live in a hovel, or you live in a penthouse on Madison Avenue (yuppie), if you don't have the heavenly, fresh-baked-goods scent wafting from your kitchen, then you aren't really home. You are just in four enclosed walls.

ICING. Whether you like to plow through it

first or savor it till the end, icing is the icing on the cake. Literally.

JOY. Unbridled.

KNIVES. Again, no need for all that messed up slicing when one person gets a huge slice and someone else, a dilapidated sliver. Cupcakes are the great leveler wherein we are all equals.

LOVE. Nothing says love like a cupcake does. If you don't bake someone a cupcake then you don't really care about them.

MOODS. There is a cupcake to fit your every mood. A diet therapist may tell you that being an emotional eater is unhealthy, and they would probably be right. But who wants to be right when you could be eating a cupcake?

NO. People say "no" too often. Cupcakes will make them say "yes."

OLIGARCHY. Vegan cupcakes will take over the world. Better to give in sooner rather than later and make this a smooth transition.

PORTABLE. You can take cupcakes anywhere. Walk down the street eating a piece of cake and you will look like a crazy person. But walk down the street eating a cupcake? Your sexiness factor will increase by at least 70 percent, according to our studies.

QUICK. Cupcakes bake very quickly and you with your busy schedule can use your newfound free time to do things that are important to you, like building a shelf for all your cupcake supplies.

RELAXING. Piping frosting from a pastry bag sets your soul at ease.

SHOPPING. You will soon find yourself perusing the baking supply stores with a purpose. Now you can admire decorating tips and pastry bags with the pros.

TRANSCENDENTAL. We will bake with our own hands; we will frost with our own icing; we will speak with our own mouths full.

UTILITARIAN. No pesky plates and forks to wash afterward. Fewer dishes, more efficiency.

VOLUPTUOUS. Doesn't your butt need a little extra padding? Sure it does.

WORKERS OF THE WORLD UNITE. Cupcakes are the fuel of the revolution. Let them eat cake. No really, let them eat cake.

XXX. Cupcakes are sexy.

YAWN. Writing A to Z lists gets very tiring. Quit reading this and start making cupcakes.

ZZZZZ. Especially when you get to Z. Now, seriously, go make some cupcakes.

"If you like sweet things (and who doesn't?) and you're vegan you are seriously missing out if this book doesn't inhabit your kitchen shelf." —SuperVegan.com

❖

"I am giving this amazing cookbook to all my friends! These beautiful cupcakes are delicious and loaded with wonderful ingredients. I can't wait to have a cupcake/champagne party so we can try them all!" —Alicia Silverstone

PRAISE FOR
VEGAN WITH A VENGEANCE

"Plenty of attitude, and killer recipes to back it up. Watch out Betty Crocker."
—Erik Marcus, Vegan.com

❖

"[Features] dairy-free desserts that are tasty enough to fool most omnivores."
—*Publishers Weekly*

❖

"Good, honest vegan recipes with broad appeal." —*Associated Press*

❖

"Creative, inventive and yummy . . . amazingly decadent desserts." —*Herbivore*

To Bea Arthur, in hopes that she will see this and give us a quote for the next book.
We love you Bea!

Copyright © 2006 by Isa Chandra Moskowitz and Terry Hope Romero
Photography copyright © 2006 by Rebecca Bent LLC

Designed by Pauline Neuwirth, Neuwirth & Associates, Inc.
Set in 10.5 point Whitman by the Perseus Books Group

Cataloging-in-Publication data for this book is available from the Library of Congress.

ISBN: 978-1-56924-273-5

Published by Da Capo Press
A Member of the Perseus Books Group
www.dacapopress.com

Da Capo Press books are available at special discounts for bulk
purchases in the U.S. by corporations, institutions, and other organizations.
For more information, please contact the Special Markets Department at the Perseus
Books Group,2300 Chestnut Street, Suite 200, Philadelphia, PA, 19103, or call
(800) 810-4145, ext. 5000, or e-mail special.markets@perseusbooks.com.

20 19 18 17 16 15 14 13 12 11

ISA CHANDRA MOSKOWITZ & TERRY HOPE ROMERO

VEGAN CUPCAKES

TAKE OVER THE WORLD

75

DAIRY-FREE RECIPES

FOR CUPCAKES

THAT RULE

Photography by Rebecca Bent

Da Capo
LIFE
LONG

A MEMBER OF THE PERSEUS BOOKS GROUP